Bad Birds 3

Yet another collection of (mostly) true stories starring the gobblers we all love to hate

By Jim Spencer

Contents

Continued, page 6

Dedication

Turkey hunting has brought me many, many lifetime friendships, and there are dozens (maybe hundreds) of folks worthy of this book's dedication. But this one is for the fourteen generous and concerned souls who met in eastern Alabama on a hot June weekend in 2020 to celebrate their friendship and reminisce about the past, but more importantly to brainstorm about possible solutions to the drastic downturn in turkey populations across the southeastern United States.

A seed was planted that weekend. Nourished by the will and determination of those 14 people, not to mention the start-up money that came out of their pockets, that seed has grown into the phenomenally successful (and still growing) organization known as Turkeys For Tomorrow, or TFT.

It is one of the proudest claims of my life to have been a part of that group and part of that initial effort. I had the honor, along with my wife Jill Easton, of serving as a founding board member of TFT. Though neither of us is still on the board, we are both strong supporters of TFT and stand in awe of the progress the organization has already made, and the many things that are in the works as I write these words, barely three years after that June 2020 meeting.

Please, go to the TFT website (www.turkeysfortomorrow.org) and check them out. Please consider becoming a member if you think it's a good organization. (I assure you it is.)

Continued, page 8

I've already mentioned that Jill and I were among the 14 folks at the initial meeting. Here, in alphabetical order, are the other 12:

David Cardin
Barry Estes
Buddy Hanks
Coates Head
Ron Jolly
Tes Jolly
Mike Lingo
Kevin Matthews
Phillip Morton
Jim Ronquest
Jeff Sherwood
Mark Yarborough

This book is dedicated to you. On behalf of turkey hunters everywhere, thank you. It's an honor to be mentioned on the same page with each and every one of you.

Foreword

By Jill J Easton

Some people are born with the DNA to become passionate turkey hunters and outdoorsmen. Jim Spencer possesses those genes. He also chose his parents well. Truman loved hunting, fishing and outdoor adventure and Rosie didn't worry much about where her skinny, outdoor-obsessed son was hanging out. On the rare occasions she fussed about it, Truman always had the same comeback:

"Leave him alone, Momma. I'd rather look for him on the creek bank than in the pool hall." Pool halls were bad hangouts for boys in the 1950s and '60s.

Truman taught his eager, non-pool hall son the basics of fishing and small game hunting, but in those days turkeys and deer were so scarce in most of eastern Arkansas that just seeing a track of either was an event told and retold at the local liars' tables.

Jim and his lifelong buddy Joe Lorinc roved the rural landscape surrounding their hometown of Stuttgart, Arkansas. The two heathens rode their bikes for miles out of town in every direction, fishing the irrigation reservoirs and canals that watered the rice fields. They hunted squirrels, ducks (of course, Stuttgart, duh,) doves, rabbits and quail. Jim trapped mink, muskrats and coons in December and January.

The Spencer family wasn't exactly poor, but there wasn't much money left at the end of the month. Jim worked as a kid, mowing yards in the summer, raking leaves in the fall, and, as mentioned, trapping in the winter. Possums brought 25 cents each, and a coon was worth the eye-popping sum of two whole dollars! When Jim put a shell into the chamber of his old Iver Johnson 20 gauge single shot (he bought them one at a time, 15 cents each, at Belcher's Hardware on Main Street,) he intended to bring something down with it.

In his mid-teens, he graduated to a 12 gauge Mossberg pump gun, and squirreled away enough money to buy a half-case (at that time, 10 boxes) of 12-gauge Winchester Mark V high-brass shells. He dumped the contents of all 10 boxes on his bed, then sat there cross-legged, running his hands through the mound of red plastic and gleaming brass like Scrooge McDuck. He says he has never felt more prosperous, before or since.

Incidentally, that's one of Jim's favorite non-turkey hunting stories, and I've heard him tell it dozens of times. When he tells it you can see the gleam in his eye. Sixty-three years after the fact, the memory of that bed full of shotgun shells still makes him feel rich.

I tell you all this to give you some idea of the death-grip the outdoors has on this man whose words you are about to read. I've never known anyone with more passion for things wild.

*　　*　　*

As much as Jim Spencer loves the outdoors, though, it wasn't until his 30th year that turkeys entered his life. Turkey populations were expanding rapidly in the 1970s, and along with them came a resurgence in interest in this grand spring pastime. Jim, being the independent cuss he is, decided to become a turkey hunter.

But turkey hunters in his neck of the woods grew few to the hill, and the few there were had lockjaw on the subject. So he bought a diaphragm mouth call at Mack's Sport Shop (which later grew into Mack's Prairie Wings.) Jim didn't even know how to position the call in his mouth, and he was too independent (read: stubborn) to ask anybody. Awash in ignorance, he went turkey hunting on his own – with predictable results.

After several years of frustration and never even getting close to killing a gobbler, he gave up, announcing that fact in a rant that appeared in his weekly newspaper outdoor column. *"Spring mornings are too valuable for fishing to waste them on imaginary creatures like turkeys,"* he wrote. A casual acquaintance named Robert Steinmetz read that column, took Jim on as a project and taught him the basics, even going so far as calling Jim's first gobbler to the gun. (It took two weekends to do it.) That was in April, 1981. Jim has never been the same.

That first gobbler wasn't much. To use Jim's own description: *"…18 pounds, an 8-inch beard not much thicker than a milkshake straw, spurs that looked like miniature Hershey's Kisses – your typical late-hatched two-year-old after a poor mast crop and a tough winter."* But it was the trophy of all trophies to this newly-blooded turkey warrior, and it was the seed of an addiction that has lasted, as of now, for 45 years and counting. Jim isn't the best caller in the woods, and he'd be the first to tell you that. Nor is he the smartest tactician. But give him a vintage Lohman box call and a shotgun and he will be out there, day after day, from the middle of March somewhere deep in Dixie to the end of May somewhere far north of the Mason-Dixon line. He is drawn to turkeys like hummingbirds are drawn to red feeders.

If you want a good illustration of what I'm telling you, try this: This spring, we hunted, in order: south Florida; Campeche, Mexico; north Arkansas; south Arkansas; southwest Colorado; northeast Kansas; and southwest Michigan – a rather short spring itinerary for us. We'd wrapped up the 2023 turkey season (or so I thought) and were driving home from Michigan. It was May 18.

"You know," Jim said casually, as we circled east of St. Louis on I-255, "Maine's turkey season goes into early June this year. That's still two weeks away, and we could…"

I cut him off. "Oh no you don't, Jimmy Buck Bob." (That's what I call him when I'm mildly annoyed. When he *really* gets me riled, that morphs into the more formal James Buckminster Robert.) I grabbed his arm and shook it for emphasis. "I'm not part of this, so there is no 'we' here. If you want to go, then go. But leave me out of it."

On May 24, six days after I called him Jimmy Buck Bob and shook his arm in western Illinois, Jim and his friend Randy Northern (also, obviously, a certified turkaholic) left for Maine. They drove three 9-hour days, hunted five days, then drove three more days to get home. During that span, they put nearly 5000 miles on Randy's vehicle, tagged three big Maine gobblers (see chapters 13 and 20) and shelled out enough money to make a down payment on a new truck.

Picture it: two 75-year-old men, both gimpy, at least one of them grumpy (that would be Jimmy Buck Bob; Randy is a nice guy,) off on a spur-of-the-moment lark that took them halfway across the country. To hear them tell it, they had the time of their lives – and I have no doubt they mean every word of it.

That's the man you bought this book from. Just so you know.

*   *   *

Jim and I came into each other's lives when we were each a year on either side of 50. (He's the older one, thank you very much.) We met at an outdoor writer's conference in 1998, in Fort Smith, Arkansas. Jim then worked for the Arkansas Game & Fish Commission. He was wearing two hats, attending the conference as an outdoor writer, but also as a representative of the AGFC, issuing complementary hunting and fishing licenses to the out-of-state radio hosts, television personalities and outdoor writers attending the event. I ask you: what damsel could avoid falling in love with a man with the extraordinary power to make Arkansas hunting and fishing free?

This slender, dark-bearded man told great stories and was easy to talk to. Over the five-day conference we developed a friendship that was cemented by two events. As a certified CPR instructor, I was doing

Jill and her first longbeard, affectionately named "Pinky." If you saw the color of the paint the taxidermist used on the legs, you'd understand.

an outdoor rescue seminar and used Jim as my CPR dummy, putting a lip-lock on him when it came time to do rescue breaths. Shortly after that he promised to take me turkey hunting to try for my first gobbler, an experience that had escaped me for nearly 15 years of off-and-on turkey hunting.

The next spring, my first turkey gobbler came to his calling on a ridge on Muddy Creek WMA, a big, rough chunk of the Ouachita National Forest in western Arkansas. After a few minutes of pure panic when Jim could see the bird and all I could see was the tip of a fanned tail, the big gobbler pivoted around and strutted into my gun sights. That turkey now hangs on a barnwood wall in our house. It is one of my proudest possessions.

Twenty-five springs have passed since that fateful shot, and Jim and I are inseparably bonded by a love of the outdoors. He's not quite so slender as before, and the dark beard now shines silver. But we still chase turkeys each spring across the country (and sometimes out of the country, too.) In a typical spring we'll hunt six to eight states, occasionally more. There are four seasons in our year: trapping, TURKEY HUNTING, fishing and firewood cutting. Bet you can't guess which is his favorite.

It's been a great quarter-century, filled with sparkling spring mornings, far distant gobbles that (sometimes) become strutting gobblers and turkey travels that are the center of our lives. If you run into us somewhere along the trail in some future spring, say howdy and tell us some turkey stories. Jim is always willing to talk about these birds he can't leave alone.

For that matter, so am I.

Chapter 1

The Orchard Tender

Probably you've never had the opportunity to hunt turkeys in a pecan orchard. If somebody invites you to do it, here's my advice: *Don't.*

Tell them you prefer to pick out your own hair shirts. I've tried several times to kill gobblers in pecan orchards, and not once has it worked out well. Like this time:

North-central Missouri, late April, perfect weather. I'd been hunting with my wife. Jill had killed a bird the day before and was taking the morning off to rest and catch up on stuff. For three days we'd been hearing a gobbler making a lot of racket a few hundred yards beyond the boundary of our hunting area, and the afternoon of that third day I went to the county courthouse, bought a plat map (this was long before OnX, HuntStand, ScoutLook and the rest) and contacted the landowner.

To my surprise, this soft-spoken man agreed to let a perfect stranger hunt his property. Said it impressed him that I'd taken the time to look him up and give him a call. I suppose odder things have happened.

But what the plat map didn't tell me, and what I'd been too surprised to ask the landowner, was what was beyond the dense woodlot that ran along the other side of the fence. I found out the next morning, going in blind, and you already know what I found.

The strip of woods was nearly a mile long but only a couple hundred yards wide, and on the far side, the pecan orchard was of the same dimensions. The trees were healthy but still fairly young, with trunks only about a foot in diameter, and the bahia and timothy ground cover hadn't had a chance to grow much. It was a turkey hunter's nightmare – flat as a roadkilled gray squirrel, way too few trees to provide enough cover for me to change positions. There wasn't a single tree big enough to provide a good set-up, and it was open enough in there for a turkey to spot you a quarter-mile away.

There's a name for stuff like that: untenable situation. But I was already in there and it was already getting light, so I made the best of it. *Maybe he'll stay in the woods*, I thought.

Things looked good at first. He started gobbling not far from the property we'd hunted for three days, and I was able to get between him and the orchard. He answered my first tree call and I shut up. I knew he'd come my way; no sense hanging him up in the tree.

But he liked hearing his own voice so much he hung his own self up, and the sun was up before he flew down. The woods were too narrow for me to move the 75 yards south that would have put me in range of his travel path, and I saw him marching slowly through the woods 100 yards away, not strutting but gobbling every five or six seconds. He passed into the orchard, marched into what appeared to be its geographical center and started strutting. Sitting at the edge of the wood line, I could see him plainly. But he refused to respond to my calls, except to face me and strut even harder.

I watched him for the next four hours, and despite me changing set-ups three times and calling from each new spot, he never moved a yard in my direction. Meanwhile, another bird was gobbling behind me on the property we'd been hunting, and at mid-morning I left the Orchard Tender and went after the other one. He was a Bad Bird, too, and he'd whipped me three days straight. Two hours later, he'd run his winning streak to four days.

The Orchard Tender was still gobbling a little, so with about 45 minutes of time left, I went back over there. Same story. When time expired at 1 p.m., he was still nailed to the ground in the middle of the orchard.

*   *   *

The next morning found me waiting in ambush about where the gobbler had entered the orchard the previous day. After he'd gobbled about 20 times, I gave him my single squeaky run of tree yelps. He gobbled back. I shut up. He flew down, earlier this time, and I hit him with a short, choppy cut-yelp. He gobbled into the back end of my call from about 150 yards. Half a minute later I saw him. This time he was strutting in the woods. I took that as a good sign, particularly since he was heading my way.

But you know how it is with turkeys. He closed to about 80 yards, and when he failed to see a hen he angled to his right, my left, and went by me at 60 yards into the orchard. I like watching turkeys strut as well as the next hunter, but I also like to shoot one every once in a while. I gave him another three hours of my life, again moving several times, and if he ever got out of a 10-foot circle I didn't see him do it.

Meanwhile, ol' Plan B was gobbling again on the other property, so I went to him again and gave him the chance to run his string to five days. He did. By the time he got through dragging me through the dirt it was so close to the closing bell I just went on back to camp. The Orchard Tender was still gobbling when I closed the door of my truck. I didn't want to hear him anymore that day.

*   *   *

The next day was Monday, the start of Missouri's second

week, and Jill's second tag was in play. We decided to double-team the orchard gobbler the next day, and when daylight came we were covering both of his previous entry points to the orchard. The cardinal, the owl and the crow all had their turns. Nothing from the Orchard Tender, though. He was taking a day off. But Plan B was in fine fettle, gobbling at everything he heard and also gobbling just for the heck of it. He gobbled over 200 times – that's where I stopped counting – before flying down and moving away out of hearing.

Meanwhile, the Orchard Tender still hadn't made a sound, but we finally heard his heavy wingbeats when he flew down. Jill and I were sitting 150 yards apart. And so help me, he threaded the needle between us, never getting within 70 yards of either of us. He entered the orchard, marched to the same spot and went through his customary show-off routine, except today he stayed as mute as the pecan tree he was strutting under.

We didn't give him three hours this time. We went after Plan B and spent the rest of the morning trying to find him. We couldn't.

*   *   *

Then it was Tuesday, our last day to hunt. We discussed several last-ditch options, and I mentioned that Preston Pittman had once dug a trench in a field to kill a difficult field bird. Or at least that's what he claims, but I know Preston and he'll lie. Regardless of veracity, though, Jill nixed the plan. It wasn't our land, and anyway, we didn't have a shovel. But we did decide to go into the orchard before daylight and set up on the biggest trees we could find within 45 yards of the Tender's strutting stage. Neither of us likes decoys, and we weren't about to resort to using one now.

Jill is slender enough that we felt she could get away with sitting against a foot-wide tree, but for me that idea is preposterous. So she sat at her tree, and when he started gobbling I made myself as comfortable as possible in a prone position beside mine.

Guess what? The Orchard Tender had itchy feet that final morning, and when he flew down he went into the adjacent property. We followed, flanked him two or three times, but every time we did he changed direction.

At 11 o'clock we threw in the towel, and when legal shooting time expired we were 50 miles down the road toward home.

To hell with pecan orchards.

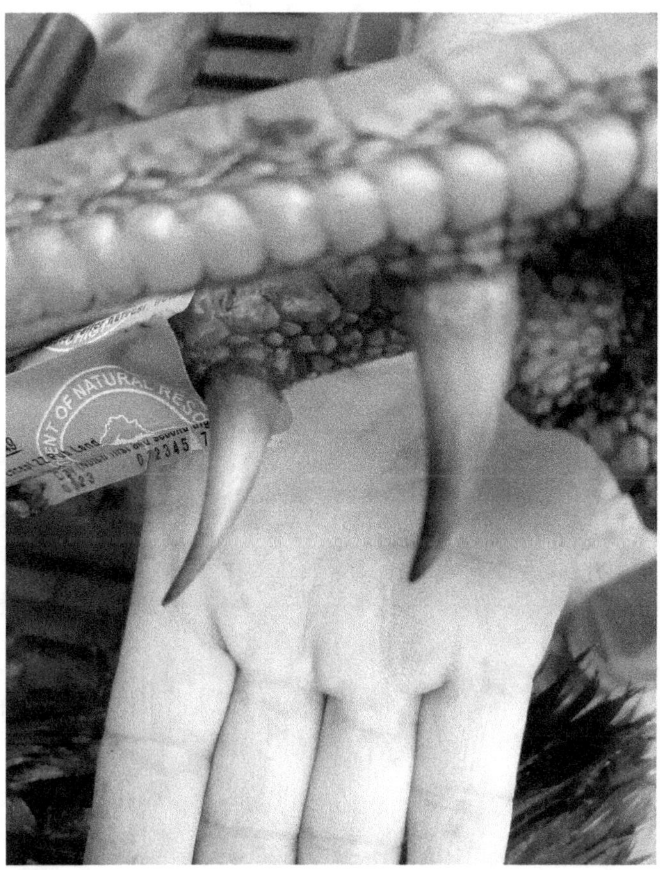

We never even came close to killing The Orchard Tender, so that means his spurs had to look something like this. Right?

Chapter 2

The Junkman

The first time we heard him was during a scouting/listening expedition a few days before the season. We know the area now, but back then we were newbies to this section of the Ozarks and were just beginning to learn our way around.

We'd left the gravel and were a half-mile in on a gated logging road, and we'd stopped to listen at an old log yard carved into a mature stand of planted shortleaf pine. The yard was reverting to forest as fast as it could. We parked there at daylight and leaned against the truck, listening. A pile of old household trash sprawled in ugly majesty at the edge of the clearing – an old stove that dated to the 1950s, a Zenith TV set complete with rabbit ears and a busted picture tube, part of a folding chair, empty cans and bottles. Typical redneck hillbilly refuse, dumped there by people whose front yards were already filled to capacity.

"It looks like a Junkman's toybox," Jill whispered, gesturing at the pile. Just then a turkey gobbled, fairly close.

"And there's the Junkman himself," I whispered back. Presto, before either of us ever hunted him, this turkey had his name.

Aside from the junkpile, this turkey lived in a great place. The 50-acre pine plantation (north of the logging road) had a closed canopy and the understory was sparse, mostly dogwoods and redbuds with a few scattered blackberry clumps where the sun reached the ground. South of the road, the land dropped off into a wide, pretty hardwood flat that was mostly level for a half-mile before narrowing and pitching into a deep, forested canyon. Beyond the canyon was a big, double-peaked mountain that rose nearly a thousand feet, with several wide, flat benches on its slopes.

The Junkman was roosted in the middle of the flat, a place we'd soon learn was one of his favored roosting areas. He didn't gobble a whole lot that morning, maybe 20 times, but at the same time we were hearing three other birds gobbling at varying distances. We marked the place on our map.

*   *   *

Two days later – the day before the opener – I went there again while Jill listened elsewhere in the national forest. All four turkeys gobbled that day, too, and The Junkman sounded like he was in the same tree. He flew down about when he was supposed to, messed around a while and then drifted south out of the roost area, gobbling enough for me to keep track. When he was far enough away, I eased into the flat to scope it out. By blind luck, I found one of his regular roost trees.

Three trees, actually. They were black cherries, stump sprouts from a tree probably logged when they cut the virgin forest more than a century ago. The stump was long gone but its coppice children were big and healthy, and they loomed over an impressive accumulation of gobbler turds. It's uncommon for turkeys to use the same roost as often as all that sign indicated, and I was excited about the find. This was a killable turkey.

Jill heard several turkeys in the places she checked, and I had a hard time talking her into hunting The Junkman with me the next morning. And when we didn't hear him nor any of the others gobble, I knew I was in for a ration of chin music from my hardcore turkey hunter bride. She didn't disappoint, and in fact, 20 years later, the topic still resurfaces on occasion.

I didn't even try to talk her into hunting him the second day of the season. She went elsewhere, but I went back and parked by The Junkman's toybox. I was early, I thought, but he was gobbling when I got there, and I didn't have far to go to get to him. He wasn't in the three black cherries but he was close, and I circled and set up along the route he'd taken when he flew down two days earlier. But today he went out the other way, into the pine plantation, and it sounded like he walked right by my truck.

It was so open out there in the pines I had to let him get farther away than I wanted before following him, but I regained a little of the lost ground by playing an unconventional card – I hid behind my big blue truck and sneaked into the log yard to keep better tabs of him. He wasn't gobbling much, but with the aid of binoculars I managed to find him. I watched him for a while, learning in the process why he had quit gobbling: he was teamed up with three hens, and he was doing his best to grin them down.

It seemed like the turkeys might keep going north to a big pasture on Forest Service land, so I backed into the flat and made a big loop around the pines, coming in on the east side of the pasture 25 minutes later. No turkeys in sight, and I didn't know if that was good or bad.

I set up a single hen decoy, something I rarely do, and backed into the cover to set up. The Junkman (I guess it was The Junkman) answered my slate call, and so did one of the hens. She sounded bitchy, so I mimicked her and she started getting worked up. Pretty soon we were in a full-blown catfight and she was getting closer.

Okay. You've heard the old advice a hundred times, and I have too. *If a gobbler has hens, try to call the hens in and the gobbler will follow.*

I was all grins when this old girl popped out of the pines into the field 75 yards away. She immediately headed my way, yawking, cutting and purring aggressively, but my grin started drooping at the ends when no gobbler followed her like the books all said he would.

She walked right past my hide and on along the edge of the field. I gave her time to either calm down or leave before I called again, but the gobbler never answered and neither did the angry hen. I hunted until noon without getting anything going.

*   *   *

About the time I was getting charged by the angry hen, Jill was pulling the trigger on one of the gobblers she'd found. It was a very nice bird, with curved spurs and a bushy beard. This disparity in our hunt results sparked another one-sided round of chin music on my wife's part. Wonderful, supportive husband that I am, I took it all in silence and good cheer. And yes, that she killed a bird that morning and I did not comes up from time to time as well.

After her trash talk wound down some, she told me there had been two other gobblers with the bird she'd killed and suggested we hunt them together the next day. Never one to turn down a gift turkey, I took her up on it. We had a close-but-no-cigar hunt on the two gobblers the next morning, and the day after that I killed one of the two but Jill couldn't get a clear shot at the other.

*   *   *

On the fifth day of the season, I went back to The Junkman by myself while Jill tried another of the turkeys she had located. This morning the bird I was after was several hundred yards south of the black cherry roost trees. He was still in the hardwood flat but was sleeping in a big, bushy open-grown pine that had grown to maturity when the area was cotton fields and pasture. It rose 30 feet above the surrounding hardwoods and The Junkman was as high in that tree as he could get.

I didn't plan it, but when I sat to the turkey I discovered I had a little visual lane up through the surrounding trees, straight to the crown of the roost tree. I could see The Junkman up there in full view, in profile. When he gobbled his beard swung away from his chest. Even at more than a hundred yards I could tell it was a bell rope. He'd been gobbling for about 10 minutes before his hens started peeping and chirping. They were about as far north of him as I was east, and I watched as they pitched out, one at a time, five of them now. This bird we had thought killable before the season was turning into something else.

As it was, the situation was untenable. The hens were already gathered under him, and he was about to pitch down into the middle of his harem. If he did that, my chances dropped off the chart.

So I got up, took a couple steps to the right to get myself out of the gobbler's sight, then walked deliberately but quietly directly at the hens. One of them picked me out right away, and they all started putting. When one flew, they all flew, mostly going west but with a couple peeling off to the north. As soon as they were gone I sat as quietly as possible beside a big white oak and waited for further developments. I was 70 yards from the base of the pine tree. I had no idea at all what might happen.

For 45 minutes, nothing did. Then the turkey gobbled, the first sound he'd made since the hens flushed. I scratched the leaves and sent out the softest, puniest run of three yelps I could coax out of my old box call. I immediately heard a limb swoosh and the sound of heavy wingbeats, and where there had been no gobbler suddenly there was one, gliding down to a clumsy, stutter-stepping halt, exactly 33 yards from my gun barrel.

When I heard the wingbeats, I laid the call down and raised my gun. When he stopped stutter-stepping and raised his head to look for the timid hen, I turned a Bad Bird into a Good Bird.

Chapter 3

The Roadside Gobblers

My first encounter with the Roadside Gobblers was accidental. I'd spent the day looking unsuccessfully for action on a large section of the Ouachita National Forest in western Arkansas, and the shadows were getting long. I was driving home on Forest Service gravel, tired, hungry, sweaty, footsore and feeling not at all charitable. It would have been a horrible time to ask me for a favor.

When I topped the gentle rise, the road was full of turkeys – a dozen or more hens, a small wad of jakes on one side, and two longbeards, one strutting, one standing respectfully in reserve, on the other. I locked the brakes and slid more or less into the middle of them. The hens and jakes went ballistic, but the two gobblers stood their ground. Both of them were up periscope, staring belligerently at my truck, and they waited until the dust settled before marching with unhurried dignity off the road and into the woods.

This was early in my turkey hunting journey, and it failed to register that I'd just performed a very good scatter. The hens had flown south, the gobblers had walked north, and I'd have had a very good chance at those gobblers if I'd had enough savvy to drive another half-mile and walk back for a hunt.

But with only three or four seasons under my belt, savvy was not yet part of my turkey hunting skill set. I drove home.

First light next morning, though, I was standing beside my truck at the top of that rise. Like many of the roads in the Ouachitas, this one ran along a narrow-topped southwest-northeast ridgeline, with a steep slope not far from each side of the road. It was a good listening place, and even with my severe savvy shortage, I at least knew that much.

When the cardinals woke up, so did the two gobblers. They were far downslope on the north side of the road, a little west of the truck. I already had my gear ready, and before they gobbled the third time I was on my way.

They were roosted in a stand of large shortleaf pines downslope from a rocky bench, and I reached the bench just as I heard them leave the trees. They weren't far, maybe 150 yards, and I hurriedly made a set that gave me a view of the bench and the slope below it. Both gobblers answered my first call.

I've already mentioned I was a few puppies short of a pet store in my turkey hunting knowledge. During the next two hours I proved it beyond the faintest doubt. Emboldened by their quick response, I immediately fired back another series of yelps. They gobbled again. I yelped again. They gobbled again. I yelped again. You get the picture. I overcalled and hung them up.

Then I heard the hens, up the slope and halfway back to the truck. The gobblers heard them, too, and they immediately started that way. They still gobbled at me, but they walked toward the real thing, and when everybody got back together the gobbling stopped.

I could still keep track of them, though, because the jakes had joined the party and every minute or two one or two of them would let out a weird yawking sound. Four decades later, I know the yawking was probably in response to drumming by one or both longbeards. I didn't know it then, but it wouldn't have mattered anyway. The big boys were knee-deep in girlfriends and I was no longer relevant.

After a while the jakes quit yawking, and after a long hour

of silence I climbed back to the truck and went elsewhere. Late that afternoon, when the shadows were long, I topped that same rise on my way home and ran into the turkeys again. The jakes were absent, but the dozen hens and two longbeards were there, within 50 feet of where I'd seen them the day before. Everybody left the road in the same direction this time, and I drove on home with a smile on my face. I'd read something recently from one of the old turkey guys – Dwain Bland, maybe? – to the effect that if he saw a gobbler do the same thing two days running, the turkey would die on the third day. I knew where I'd be late the next afternoon.

*   *   *

I took my camo clothes and hunting stuff to work the next day, and at quitting time I was first out the door. I arrived 90 minutes early, glassed the road from a half-mile away. Good news: no turkeys in sight. I changed into my camo on the side of the road, hot-footed it through the woods paralleling the road and set up within shotgun range of the gravel. I'd planned to just sit and wait, but I couldn't resist doing just a little calling. And before I knew it, my inexperienced eagerness overtook me and "just a little" ballooned into something you'd expect to hear during the warm-up before a turkey calling contest.

Wouldn't you know it, I called in the jakes. They're protected in Arkansas now, but then they were fair game, and I was both surprised and proud when I decided not to shoot. The gobblers would be along presently, I told myself smugly.

The youngsters milled around as jakes will do, grab-assing aimlessly amongst themselves, but I was well hidden and they didn't pick me out. An hour later they were still milling around in the road when a gobble erupted so close behind me I'm still surprised its author didn't see me flinch. The jakes snapped upright and stopped their tomfoolery, and all of us, the four jakes and me, were as motionless as

Jim Spencer

Kaw-Liga. (Google it, all you under-40 children. It's a classic Hank Sr. song.)

Anyway…a little while later there was another gobble, this one 75 yards west, and a few seconds after that the two longbeards stepped into the road. One of them gobbled again, and down the slope on the south side of the road a hen fast-yelped in response.

Within minutes there were 17 turkeys in the road – 11 hens, the four jakes and both longbeards – but the only ones in range were the jakes. Again I held off; it's what I do nowadays, but it still surprises me that I did it then, with less than a dozen turkeys to my credit and my bloodthirsty quotient still red-lined.

My confidence that the longbeards would eventually work themselves into shotgun range was misplaced. They stayed 60 to 80 yards away until almost sundown, at which time they followed the hens off the road and down the north slope.

*   *   *

Next afternoon, I was 30 yards closer to where the turkeys left the road, but it didn't matter because I was the only one who showed up that day. Wednesday afternoon I was there again, and again nobody else showed. Thursday and Friday I gave us all a rest. Saturday morning's first light found me at the rise in the road, standing beside my truck drinking coffee, waiting for the first cardinal. The gobblers beat the redbird to the punch, sounding off at a barred owl's ancient question just as the east was showing its first glow. They were about where I thought they'd be on the north slope, and I was able to get there both quietly and in plenty of time to pick out a good tree about a hundred yards from the roost.

But complications quickly came to light. I was barely settled in when a sleepy hen conversation started in the trees past the gobblers. Bad news.

Predictably, the hens flew down first and walked to the gobblers. The big boys flew down to them, and I could see the whole mob milling around on the ground 80 yards away. I watched the dominant gobbler top two hens, and then the whole flock started away from me along the bench. I let them get out of sight, then climbed the slope and made a try at getting ahead of them but lost them somehow in the transition.

I never made contact again that morning, but I'd brought plenty of groceries and water and I simply stayed put. I was sitting beside the road that afternoon when they came out. The longbeards were 60 yards away and slowly closing, and I had my gun shouldered and the safety off when I heard gravel popping far down the road. The turkeys stopped moving toward me and listened to the approaching vehicle, and soon two blue-haired ladies in a dusty black sedan came over the rise and drove into the turkeys, same as I'd done the previous weekend and with similar results. Turkeys went every which way, the car kept on going, and I stayed until dark but heard and saw nothing.

The next morning nobody gobbled or yelped within hearing distance of the rise in the road, and when I arrived in the afternoon for one last vigil, I found two red 12 gauge hulls in the road, 30 yards from two scattered circles of black-tipped feathers and a few drops of still-tacky blood in each circle.

Chapter 4

Brigham

"Good Lord, look at that mess of hens he's got with him!" said John Spore, squinting through his binoculars. The gobbler was strutting in an alfalfa field not far from Eureka, Kansas. Moving slowly through the greenery ahead of him were, by actual count, 21 hens. Two jakes were also in attendance, but every time either got too close to a hen, the strutter was quick to put a stop to it.

We were on the edge of a plateau, looking down at the turkeys. The high ground was part of the Flint Hills and we were only about 100 feet above the alfalfa field, but it seemed much higher. The steep slope between us and the turkeys was studded with rocks from baseball to boulder size and cloaked with big, gnarly hardwoods, mostly bur oak and hickory but other stuff, too – locust, black gum, sycamore, hackberry. The mixed canopy was thick enough to hide us as we dropped to the edge of the field, and we moved along the base of the ridge until we located the flock again.

They were 200 yards away when we found them, and I suggested we sit down and give them a try.

"What's the use?" John asked. "What can we offer him he hasn't already got? Right now he's the richest gobbler in the world. He's standing in 40 acres of the best groceries a turkey can have, and he's got more wives than Brigham Young." This turkey wasn't a Bad Bird (not yet, anyway) but he already had a name.

John was exaggerating a little bit – that horny old Mormon had more than 50 wives – but his point was still valid. Just what, exactly, did we have to offer this gobbler who had 21 ladies?

But, there's this: an old baseball coach once told me if you aim at nothing, you're sure to hit it, and a slim chance is still a chance. Sure, the richest gobbler in the world didn't have much to gain – who in the world needs 22 wives? – but neither did we have much to lose. So we left the shelter of the trees and crawled through the tall grass bordering the field. There was nothing to lean against, but the grass hid us well, and it was a comfortable enough setup if you discounted the chiggers we'd be dealing with later.

We decided that with all the competition out there in the field, we'd better make a pretty good showing with our calling. We launched into a spirited concert, each of us running two calls at once and mixing it up as best we could, playing off one another's calling, running yelp sequences up into loud bursts of cutting. I had a pair of those brand-new Knight & Hale push-button Fighting Purr calls, and I threw some of that into the mix as well.

It created a pretty good stir out there in the alfalfa. Several of the hens, which until then had been peacefully feeding and ignoring the strutting longbeard, started moving around and messing with each other. The jakes got all hot and bothered and started chasing each other and yawking. One of them choke-gobbled a couple times, sounding like he had alfalfa caught in his throat. And the longbeard, which hadn't gobbled since we had first seen him, broke silence and gobbled a half-dozen times during our two-minute serenade.

But none of the turkeys moved in our direction. When we stopped calling, they started gradually settling down, like waves on a lake when the wind quits blowing. Pretty soon everything was back to normal.

We waited five minutes and did it again.

And the turkeys got revved up again. Hens chased hens, jakes played tag and tried to gobble, longbeard repeatedly announced he was in charge around here, so everybody just behave. Toward the end of our encore performance, the jakes started moving our way.

You know how jakes are when they get worked up. They came fast, like puppies trying to beat each other to the dog food bowl, shouldering their way past each other in turn as they trotted across the field. Not wanting them to lose purpose and stop, we kept pouring it on and they kept coming. When they were 50 yards from us, the longbeard couldn't stand it anymore. He headed our way, too.

He came twice as fast as the jakes, determined to put them back in their place and enlarge his harem at the same time. But he didn't come fast enough. What looked like a miracle in the making turned to tragedy, faster than you can read about it. The longbeard was still 80 yards out when the jakes arrived literally at our feet. We quit calling when they were still 30 yards away, but I don't think they even realized it. They pushed and shoved the rest of the way until we could have, no fooling, touched them with our gun barrels.

We didn't have time to engage in such foolishness, though. At a range of four feet, one of the jakes made eye contact with me. I knew better than to look him in the eye, because turkeys don't like making eye contact with predators. Especially when said predators are close enough to peck. But I couldn't help it, you know?

Predictably, all hell broke loose. The young gobbler let out with a loud, shrill sound I've never heard from a turkey, before or since. Neither cluck nor yelp nor putt, it was a noise that could be mistaken for nothing but what it was: a sound of pure, unadulterated terror. The jake drew it out over two full seconds, during which time he executed a 180 and charged back from whence he'd come. He reversed directions so fast he and his buddy collided chest to chest, and they went down in a tangle of legs, wings and necks. They quickly regained their feet and were instantly airborne, beating it out of there like they'd seen a cougar. The wingwash was so close and strong I felt my cap lift off my forehead.

The longbeard, now inside 60 yards, turned on a dime, harem forgotten, and sprinted back across the field. He ran by the hens at top speed, and they took off running behind him. Within 60 seconds, probably somewhat less, that alfalfa patch was as empty of turkeys as a Dollar General parking lot. I looked over at John.

"Well," he said, pulling his mask off and straightening his glasses, "that was interesting." A master of understatement, was my old friend John.

*   *   *

We had other places to hunt, so we let the alfalfa field rest the next morning. But when we drove by there about noon, with John's gobbler riding with us, the big flock of hens was out there again. Faithfully guarding them was old Brigham, but we didn't see the jakes. Maybe we'd scared them to death.

It was hot and so were we, and we had John's gobbler to deal with. So for the moment we left the turkeys to their own devices. But late that afternoon we drove by for another look-see. They were still out there, but they'd moved closer to the far end of the field, where it started necking down as the high ground started crowding the creek that formed the north border of the field.

This was good news, provided we could get to the end of the field ahead of the turkeys. We drove out of sight and parked, then climbed to the top of the high ground and hot-footed the half-mile to the end of the field. Easing over to the edge, we finally spotted the turkeys, still 100 yards from where the field ended. We couldn't see Brigham through the thick vegetation on the hillside, but we did see eight or nine hens and figured he was still tending them.

We moved a couple hundred yards more and fell off the hill.

When we got to the creek, we sneaked downstream along the bank until we could see the field opening up in front of us. It took us 15 minutes to cover the next 50 yards, and we stopped when John spotted the first hen. We were still 30 yards from the field, and she was 30 yards beyond that.

Taking advantage of the vegetation and the deep shade, we dropped to our knees and crawled five yards to the nearest decent tree, a big sycamore growing on the bank of the creek. It was wide enough for two people, and since it was right on the creek, it was also on the natural silt/loam levee that flanks most alluvial streams. It wasn't much of a rise, but it gave us another foot of altitude, and that's important on a turkey set-up.

We didn't call at first. The hens were still feeding contentedly, and by now we'd found the gobbler. His jake buffoons were back, and he'd picked up a satellite longbeard who was also strutting some. The closest hens were almost to the field edge, and the two longbeards were 25 yards behind. The problem was, we were running low on daylight.

John purred on a crystal pot and peg, and I clucked and whined with a mouth call. We needed something to happen, and fast. Some of the hens raised their heads and peered into the gloom of the woods, but as far as we could tell the gobblers had no reaction. Two minutes later, the hens started flying up from the field, coming into the woods with us to roost. Two of them lit in our sycamore tree.

The gobblers stood pat for a couple more minutes, and then, with daylight leaving fast, they marched away from us along the edge of the field and flew up – the two longbeards first, then the jakes – into several other sycamores maybe 200 yards away. Game over.

Well…not quite over. We were pinned down like kindergarten drawings on a refrigerator, underneath God knows how many hen turkeys, and there was little chance of sneaking out of there without spooking them. But we still had a play left. We could spook the hens on purpose and hope they'd go in the opposite direction from the gobblers.

We worked out the details in whispers, then stood up at the same time and started talking in normal voices. "Let's go straight to the edge of the field and shoot from there," I said.

"Okay, let's go," John answered. When our boots touched alfalfa, we fired two shots each into the air, with five Mississippis between shots. Nothing happened with the first shot, but at the second things started happening. Turkeys flew in every direction – across the creek, upstream along the creek, up the ridge to the high ground. Two of them even flew out over our heads and sailed across the field to the woods beyond. The gobblers and jakes were far enough away that they didn't fly, or at least we didn't hear them if they did.

"Well, I think that was a decent scatter," John said. "I hope it helps us in the morning."

*   *   *

Nineteenth century poet Emily Dickenson once wrote that "Hope is the thing with feathers." But not this time. We were careful to get there well before daylight and put out two decoys, jake and hen, along the field edge not far from where we'd shot the night before. Neither John nor I liked using decoys, but we figured there would be a certain amount of confusion in the field that morning. With that many lonesome hens for competition, we figured we'd need them.

We weren't certain the gobblers had stayed put during all the racket we'd made, but when they started gobbling at cardinal time they were right there. Since there were no hens close by to answer, they gobbled a lot.

Breaking my self-imposed rule about not calling much to roosted gobblers, I answered them with a couple tree calls, then a fly-down cackle, then a series of louder yelps and clucks. I wanted to be the first hens they heard that morning. John chimed in with a few yelps of his own. The gobblers, 175 yards away across the field, walked all over the noise we were making, and it wasn't long before we saw them sail out into the mist-shrouded field.

There's something about watching a mature turkey gobbler sail off his roost that grabs a piece of my soul. Every time I see it is the first time I ever saw it, and every time it makes my hair stand on end. The two longbeards launched at the same time and glided our way, see-sawing their wings like crop-dusters saying hello to a friend on the ground. They landed side by side, 80 yards into the alfalfa, and stared suspiciously at our little jake/hen spread.

The two jakes launched then, and soon all four were standing within 30 yards of each other, looking at the decoys. The longbeards gobbled. The jakes started walking toward us, and seconds later so did Brigham and his buddy. *I'll be dipped,* I thought. *This is actually going to work.*

Don't count your chickens, as the old saying goes. It applies to turkeys as well, as illustrated by what happened next:

The gobblers were closing in behind the jakes as they got closer, and the young birds knew it. At 60 yards the youngsters put on the brakes and parted, and the longbeards marched between them like the royalty they were. This was pre-TSS, and we were waiting for them to break the 40-yard mark when the jake decoy fell over. Just fell over, for no apparent reason. It was calm, the ground was soft and I was sure I'd pushed the stake in properly. But one second it was staring the hen decoy down, and the next second it was taking a nap beside her.

If the jakes had still been leading, it might have ended differently. But they weren't, and it didn't. When the decoy went down, their heads went up, and their feet stopped carrying them our way. John and I were down on our guns, ready to execute the one-two-three-boom, but the turkeys were still right at 50 yards away. We had a desperate, whispered conversation, decided regretfully that yes, they were too far, and watched helplessly as old Brigham re-adjusted his wings. The kiss of death. When his running buddy did it, too, we knew the hunt was blown.

The gobblers stayed in the alfalfa, but they moved a long tee shot away from where we wanted them to be. The hens reassembled one or two at a time and within an hour the big happy family was back together again. We watched them for several hours, hoping against hope. The sky, which had been cloudy and threatening all morning, finally opened up at ten o'clock. Drenched and grumpy, we gathered our stuff and called it a day.

*   *   *

I had one more morning to hunt before having to go home to Arkansas and get back to making a living, and my two Kansas tags were getting pretty heavy. I really, really wanted to hunt Brigham that last morning, but even a fool makes the right decision now and then. We hunted a different property that last day, and I lowered the hammer on a very good gobbler that gave us the show all turkey hunters want to see. He gobbled well, strutted prettily, was moderately stubborn but eventually came one yard too close. He had a good beard and beautiful, ivory-tipped curved spurs, and he weighed 22 pounds.

He was a perfect turkey in every respect save one: He wasn't Brigham.

Chapter 5

Darren's Demon

I'm pretty sure Darren put me on this particular turkey on purpose. He swears otherwise, but he's a turkey hunter and therefore, by definition, a liar. You decide:

Jill and I were in Ohio for our first time, hunting the easternmost part of the Wayne National Forest and leaning on our friend Darren Dye's intimate knowledge of the area. He'd taken us on a late-afternoon reconnaissance run the day we arrived.

"Park at this gate," he said. "Walk up the road until you reach a fork, it's about a mile, and listen from there. The left fork takes you into a big chunk of good public hunting, and the right fork goes a half-mile and hits a big food plot. If you don't hear anything, I'd check out the right fork first. Turkeys like that food plot."

Jill hunted with Darren the next day and I parked at the gate alone. Darren is a lanky, long-legged ridgerunner 25 years my junior, so it probably didn't occur to him to mention that the mile between the gate and the fork was a steep climb. I'd allowed 20 minutes for the walk, but it took me 30. When I finally reached the listening spot, multiple turkeys were already gobbling in both directions.

I stood there for a couple minutes, telling myself it was because I wanted to listen and decide on the best direction to go. The truth was, I badly needed a breather. But turkeys were gobbling hard both left and right, and I decided to go right because of what Darren said about the food plot. Also, the turkeys were closer. Also, the road wasn't as steep going that way.

The three turkeys that had been gobbling over there flew down while I was still hiking toward them. By the time I got close enough to think about setting up, only one was still talking. I could see a brighter area ahead, and I figured it would be the edge of the food plot Darren had mentioned. It looked to be about 300 yards ahead, and the turkey was gobbling between me and the brighter woods.

I didn't like the situation. If the turkey came, he'd have the sun at his back and I'd be facing the glare. But the road paralleled a deep ravine on the left and a steep bluffy rise on the right, and circling around him was out of the question. Anyway, he was probably too close to the edge of the woods to get between him and the food plot without bumping him.

It was a beautiful place, though, and when I sit down to long odds, somehow it helps if the scenery is nice. The turkey was pretty wound up on this cool, crisp morning, and he lost no time answering my first run of yelps. I was sitting close beside the logging road I'd traveled to reach the turkey, and I could see a good 150 yards down the road. A very short while after he gobbled, he stepped into the road at the limit of my line of sight. Even at that distance I could see he had a good beard.

The turkey stood erect and alert, looking my way, and he held the pose for several minutes. Then he dropped into strut, held that for another minute or two, slicked down and gobbled. Then he came up straight and tall again. I couldn't do anything but watch. I'd removed my mouth call to get a drink of water a few minutes earlier, and I'd forgotten to stick it back in my mouth. The gobbler was a good distance away, but there was nothing between us but air. And I've already mentioned he had the sun at his back. Moving to pick up the mouth call or operate a friction call would be risky.

The turkey gobbled once more, experimentally, and when nothing answered he turned his back and walked out of sight over a slight rise in the road. I waited 15 minutes, then dropped a few feet off the road down the side of the ravine and worked my way along beside the road until I reached the rise. I got my shotgun at high port and eased forward until I could see the road beyond. No turkey.

I'd been right about the brighter section of forest. It was the edge of the food plot. Looking down the road past the rise, I could see the edge of the opening less than 100 yards ahead. It was evident the land dropped off just beyond the tree line, but I couldn't tell how steep the slope was. I didn't want to blunder up there and bump the gobbler, so I followed his earlier example and called experimentally. I got exactly the same result the gobbler had gotten: nothing.

I waited a just-in-case five minutes, then eased up the road to the edge of the woods, covering the last few yards as slow as a terrapin. The field came into view a yard at a time, and at about the 75th yard, there he was, strutting in the green grass. He had four hens in front of him and a jake playing his court jester role to perfection.

I was in the shade of a big tree trunk, screened by a low-hanging dogwood limb, so I stood there and watched the show. A turkey hunter never gets tired of it. Nobody seemed in any hurry to do anything – nowhere to go, all day to get there, nothing to do after they arrived. After 45 minutes the little group of birds was still within 50 feet of where they'd been when I first spotted them. The longbeard hadn't gobbled, the four hens gave no sign they were aware of him, and the jake never quit being the jester.

It was all very entertaining and I wasn't bored, but I wasn't getting anywhere either. I needed to jump-start something. Since I haven't had much luck calling gobblers back to somewhere they've already left, I backed out, moved north along the tree line to get ahead of the flock, and eased back toward the field until I could see a couple of the hens. I made a standing set, leaning against the trunk of a big black cherry with my gun braced against the tree and on my shoulder, then raked a few coarse yelps off the gobbler side of my 30-year-old Lohman box call. The two hens I could see raised their heads and looked my way. The gobbler I couldn't see gobbled, the first time he'd done so in more than an hour. Encouraging, but a long way from confidence-inspiring.

But in a little while I noticed the two hens had moved a few yards closer, and now I could see three of them. I called again. They looked my way again. The longbeard gobbled again. The jake went *yawwwwk-yawk.* The fourth hen moved into view.

Hmmm. Maybe we were getting somewhere. I readjusted my contact with the tree trunk, trying to find a more comfortable position. The hens had closed to 35 yards. The whole time I'd been watching the turkeys interact, the gobbler had stayed within 15 yards of the hens. If that was still true, he'd be killable when I was able to see him. The hens inched forward a few more yards. I clucked and purred as softly as I could. They looked. The longbeard gobbled. The jake yawked. I was officially jacked up. I was within minutes of killing this turkey.

That's when it all fell apart. I caught a flash of brown movement with my left eye, within 15 yards of the out-front hen, and the brown movement morphed into a big coyote in full charge, rushing through the foot-high green grass he'd somehow hidden himself in. The hens blew into the air with a loud commotion of putts and cackles, and the still unseen longbeard shock-gobbled once and went away somewhere. The coyote stood there in the grass, his tongue hanging out like he'd run five miles. I could have killed him but I didn't. As a fellow turkey hunter, I identified with him. I've also stood turkeyless with my tongue hanging out.

*   *   *

Darren said he could put me in a different spot the next morning, but I declined. This second morning I knew what I was up against and allowed plenty of extra time to get in there. I was standing where the road entered the food plot well before the first cardinal chirped. Only two turkeys gobbled in there this morning, but when they did I was in a good position. They were close together in a clump of oaks at the head of a small hollow, 150 yards north of where the coyote episode took place. I only needed to move 60 yards to get between the gobblers and the food plot, and I set up where I could shoot to both the edge of the plot and the rim of the hollow. Both were in the 35 to 40 yard range.

I let them gobble a while, and then uttered a faint set of two tree yelps. The gobblers, which had been sounding off every 15 to 20 seconds, shut up. That was okay; it told me they'd heard me and were now mulling things over in their pecan-sized turkey brains. Now it was a waiting game until they came to the ground.

Which they did, after 20 minutes of silence. I heard two heavy birds leave the trees, two heavy birds thump the ground, and one turkey gobble. Mmm hmmm. The longbeard and the jake. They were still in the hollow, but from the sound of it they were just barely below the rim. If they popped up it would be a 35-yard shot. Perfect.

I hadn't used a slate yesterday, so that's what I started with today. The turkey waited about five seconds before answering my first run of yelps. Mildly interested, but not slobberingly hot. I gave him time to gobble some more or move toward me or something, but he didn't. I yelped again and he answered, but he'd moved off down the hollow instead of coming my way like a good turkey, and when he gobbled again it was obvious he was leaving.

Okay, I'd played this game before. I backed out, got back to the road I'd walked in on and ran like a crippled bear back toward the fork in the road where I'd started the hunt the first day. I got ahead of the gobbler, went down into the hollow he was traveling, and found a good set-up location. He gobbled at about 200 yards and again a few minutes later at 150. His line of travel was going to miss me, so I called to him one time to adjust his course. The next time he gobbled he was 250 yards away, going back up the hollow away from me.

I climbed back to the road and galumphed back along the road toward the food plot. I got ahead of him again, plunked down close to where I'd been sitting, waited until he gobbled again, then called to him. He gobbled back at me from 150 yards, then gobbled again five minutes later from 250. Evidently I am a slow learner.

Nothing for it but to try to get ahead of him one more time, so here I went down the road again, huffing and puffing like the little engine that could. He gobbled as I went by him, giving me a good fix, and after another 200 yards I slipped off the road and back into the hollow. As quickly and quietly as possible, I found a decent tree and settled in, promising myself this time I wouldn't call no matter what.

My heart rate was just about back to normal when I saw him coming. He was 125 yards up the hollow, walking and pecking. His hens and jake were nowhere to be seen. The hollow was wider this far down from the head, close to 100 yards across, and in my haste to get set up I hadn't gone far enough to be able to cover the whole width of the thing. I was 30 yards from the south slope, leaving a space of more than 60 yards between me and the rise on the north side of the hollow. The gobbler was skirting along the north side, and if he continued he was going to go past me ten yards out of range.

I waited long as I could to see if he was going to alter his course. When it was obvious he was going to miss me I weighed my options: Don't call and let him walk by, or try to turn him. No-brainer. When I purred he stopped for a second, then took three more purposeful steps that put him behind a big tree. That was the last I saw of him that day, and Darren's Demon had earned his name.

*   *   *

The third day the Demon had reunited with his jake and they

were again roosted in the head of the hollow. I was waiting by the food plot for the first gobble, and when it came I tree yelped, waited for him to gobble, and then did a decent fly-down cackle. Then I walked quickly back down the road toward the fork, got a couple hundred yards away from the turkeys and slipped into the hollow. This time I sat where I could cover the entire width, but it made no difference. The turkeys stayed in the tree until well after sunrise. I saw one of them pitch out going north, after which there was no turkey action for the rest of the morning.

*   *   *

The fourth and last morning in Ohio, I was in there again, waiting by the edge of the food plot. The two gobblers cranked up right about where I expected them to, but 30 or 40 yards farther down the hollow this time. It was a good development. This little extra bit of wiggle room allowed me to get close enough to the lip of the hollow to be able to partially see into it, but I still had a blind spot directly in front where the slope prevented me from seeing the ground.

As always, I had a mouth call in my cheek, but I never laid a hand on any of my other calls. I didn't use the mouth call, either, despite the exuberant gobbling of the Demon and his little buddy. From my new position, I could clearly see the tree the gobblers were in, but I never saw them until they pitched out at normal fly-down time. They glided to the ground in my direction, angling slightly to the right. They landed in my blind spot and I got my gun up.

The longbeard gobbled twice while he was out of sight, and then I caught a movement to the left of the blind spot. The jake came out of the hollow onto the flat space between the hollow and the food plot. He gave me the stink-eye but kept walking, passing out of the woods into the food plot and out of sight down the slope. As soon as he was out of sight I shifted my gun to cover where he'd popped up.

Nothing happened. I waited. Still nothing. I could feel that mouth call in my cheek, and the urge to use it was almost overwhelming. So much so, in fact, that before my willpower dissolved completely I spit the thing out into my face mask.

My gun was still aimed at where the jake had been. And then there he was, 25 yards beyond the bead of my shotgun, like Scotty had just beamed him down from the Enterprise. I don't know how turkeys do that. However he did it, though, my gun was already on him and the safety was off. All I had to do was stroke the trigger, and I somehow managed to not screw it up.

When I told Darren the story later, he immediately went to his workbench and made me a special mouth call. "Try this one on your next hunt," he said, straight-faced, handing it to me. "I think it's just what you need."

It doesn't have any reeds.

Chapter 6

The Cavemen

The cave entrance is at the high end of a beautiful hardwood flat. The flat lies between two gently sloping hillsides. Looking out from the cave entrance, the visual effect is of a wooded trough 60 yards wide, leading straight ahead (south.) The ground is level for a hundred yards before falling gently and turning 90 degrees west. If you walk across the flat and follow the trough around the bend and downhill, the valley (they call 'em "hollers" in these parts) gets wider and slightly steeper as you go. But the hardwoods stay tall, stately and pretty as far as you can see, and a good deal farther.

The cave is only a mile north of our house. Nowadays, the entrance is barricaded against human entry to protect bats or blind white fish or cave crickets or unicorns or something, but before the feds blocked it, we often took visitors there on amateur spelunking forays. One fine Halloween afternoon Jill took some friends there, and at the cave entrance they flushed a big flock of longbeards. Nobody got an exact count, but everybody agreed there were easily ten to twelve birds, maybe a few more.

The visitors wanted to see the cave, so Jill didn't take time to look around then. But when everybody left two days later, we went back to check it out. There was a good white oak mast crop that year, and the ground in front of the cave looked like a mad gardener had been there with a tiller and a cooler full of Red Bulls. You literally could not take a step without your foot landing in turkey scratching. The churned leaves continued downhill and around the curve, and as far as we could see down the slope as the holler widened. The flock of gobblers had been busy, and it looked like they had some help.

We thought about those birds all winter. A couple times we went in there to keep tabs, finding fresh sign every time. In late March we went there several times to listen, and located what we think was nine gobbling turkeys in the two-mile run of that holler. Most of them were stacked into the upper half-mile, close by the cave entrance.

We were hunting in Texas when the season opened at home, so we didn't get to the Cavemen until the fourth day of the season. It had rained hard the day before the home opener, and we were both surprised and pleased to find no fresh vehicle tracks in the muddy spots on the road leading to the cave.

*   *   *

The cave entrance has an overhanging rock formation, and that's where we stopped to listen just as the first hint of dawn was glowing in the east. Before, we'd always heard the turkeys in the holler, but this morning two answered my first owl hoot from uphill, behind us on the mountainside above the cave.

It was an unexpected direction, but not a hunt-wrecker, and when nothing gobbled in the holler in the next few minutes, we retreated the quarter-mile to the truck and went up the mountain from there, wanting to get behind and above the gobblers. The mountain was flat on top, and from the sound of it the gobblers were roosted on the front edge of that flat. Our path would take us to the opposite side, and we'd be in good position if the turkeys didn't pitch off the mountain.

The climb was steep but short, and when we reached the top we figured we were 125 yards from the turkeys. They were still in the tree. The timber on top, if you could call it timber, was scattered, stunted, spindly post oaks, all less than 10 inches in diameter. Poor set-up trees, to say the least. But there was scattered chunk rock 20 yards closer to the gobblers, and we used the last of the fading night to get to the rocks and find places to sit. It wasn't the best set-up we'd ever made, but maybe it would be good enough.

The two gobblers had a fine old time that morning. They gobbled with abandon at each other and at two distant cousins on the next ridge over, and we couldn't hear any hen talk. Even so, as sparse as the cover was between us and them, it would have been risky to call at that point. Now that the light was good, we could plainly see them in a scruffy, wind-twisted shortleaf pine on the edge of the flat. There wasn't enough vegetation between us to hide a cat squirrel, let alone two humans. So we sat still and kept quiet, waiting for developments.

The gobblers were in no hurry to fly down. I half-expected them to sail down into the head of the holler in front of the cave, but instead they pitched our way, landing about 50 yards from Jill and 60 from me. While they were getting their land legs sorted out I shifted my mouth call into place and made three soft yelps. Both turkeys spun to face the sound. Both gobbled. One of them immediately started our way, but his buddy stood fast.

Jill and I have hunted together a lot and we try to double when we get the opportunity, but we're not stupid about it. The gobbler was walking straight at us but the other hadn't moved an inch, and since Jill was almost directly between the gobblers and me I was out of the play. When the bird broke the 30-yard circle I clucked to stop him. He obliged, and Jill laid him down.

The other turkey took wing at the shot, flew over the edge of the flat and dropped out of sight. We figured he landed somewhere in or near the head of the cave holler. Jill tagged her bird and we took him to the truck, then sat there long enough to eat some crackers and split an energy drink. About 45 minutes after Jill pulled the trigger, we walked the quarter-mile along the trail that led to the cave.

We stopped 50 yards short of the cave overhang and I pointed at my hunting partner. Jill pulled out the box call she'd used to call in The Gift Bird for me more than a decade earlier (see Chapter 40 in *Bad Birds 2* for that story.) The yelps sounded good, raspy and pleading, but nobody answered. We waited a couple minutes and she called again. Nothing. We eased forward until we could see into the flat in front of the cave, and after giving it a thorough binocular examination we dropped down to the flat. We were halfway to the drop-off and bend that marked the head of the holler when a gobbler blasted out of an ash tree right above us and sailed back over our heads, landing somewhere on the mountainside above the cave. Maybe it was the bird we'd seen with Jill's turkey, maybe it wasn't. Either way he was gone, and rather than further booger any other turkeys that might be nearby, we decided to try our luck elsewhere since it was still early in the day. We hunted hard most of the day, but despite visiting four different "elsewheres", we never got anything going.

*   *   *

The next morning Jill wanted to hunt one of her favorite places, and I went back to the cave alone. One gobbled in the dark while I was getting my vest out of the truck, and I soon figured out he was just around the bend of the flat in front of the cave. By hugging the right side of the flat I used the contour of the hillside and the gloom of pre-dawn to get pretty close to him. When I sat down I was within shotgun range of his roost tree and almost at eye level with his position in it.

Getting that close was a mistake, but I was already there before I realized it. Just like the day before, I was too exposed to risk calling. At that close range and at his level on the hillside, he'd be suspicious at not seeing the hen. So I waited quietly – like the day before – and when he flew down and landed he was more than 100 yards away. Because of my elevation on the hillside I could see him plainly, but he wasn't interested in coming back to his roosting area. He gobbled a couple times at my calling but eventually drifted away down the holler.

When I could get away with it, I climbed higher on the ridge and paralleled his route of travel. I got well ahead of him, descended to the bottom and set up while he was still 200 yards uphill, coming slowly toward me and gobbling just enough to let me keep track.

I think I'd have killed him that day if I'd had the sense to just sit there and wait. He was maybe 150 yards out when he gobbled again, and it seemed to me he was angling a little wide of the mark. On his new course I'm pretty sure he'd have still been in range, but I got antsy and clucked a couple times to line him up again. That was the last I heard of him that day. I sat there with my gun on my knee for more than an hour. He was a no-show. I laid my gun back in my lap and sat there grumbling, and I guess I must have dozed off. Because next thing I knew another 45 minutes had passed and three deer were in the holler behind me, snorting and blowing. There wouldn't be any killing this turkey this day.

I had a writing deadline looming – poor planning on my part to have a deadline during turkey season, but there it was anyway – so I rested both myself and the turkey the next morning, and then Jill wanted me to come help her double-team the Bad Bird she'd been fooling with for two days. I didn't contribute anything to her hunt, and her turkey won the day for the third time.

*   *   *

I was back at the cave overhang well before listening time the next morning. Jill's turkey had gotten under her skin and she was laying in there with him, so once again I had nobody to watch my six.

53

Which was exactly the direction from which the damned turkey came to my calling that morning.

The day started on an optimistic note. I got in there early and stayed on the ridge above the holler, walked 400 yards past the normal roosting area and dropped to the bottom. I wanted to be downstream from the turkey, and he seemed to like roosting close to the cave entrance. Sure enough, when he started gobbling he was back toward the cave, maybe 200 yards away. I was starting to move his way when another gobbler cranked up behind me, downstream, also about 200 yards.

Ha! Catbird seat. The two gobblers were answering each other, and I figured there was a better than even chance they'd get together, probably somewhere close to where I was standing. Just a few yards away, a big, leafy limb had calved off its parent red oak and fallen just right, leaving a four-foot space between itself and the tree trunk. The dry leaves still clinging to the limb gave me good cover up to my shoulders. The natural blind was in the bottom of the holler, 25 yards from the north side and 45 yards from the south side. By facing the south side of the holler with a turkey straight off each shoulder, I could cover both uphill and downhill approaches, with the entire bottom of the holler in gun range. It was a sweet set-up. I was directly between two hard-gobbling turkeys, had a better blind than I could have built in a week, and could cover every approach.

The turkeys gobbled a hundred times each, came to the ground almost simultaneously, and started working their way toward each other. This thing was getting better and better. Smack between the turkeys, I sat behind my leaves and grinned like a skunk eating yellowjackets. I was certain the up-the-holler gobbler was the one I'd been fooling with, but it was the down-the-holler bird that seemed likely to get there first. Didn't matter to me, just so long as somebody came to play. I shifted most of my attention downstream and scrooched a little more to the right on my tree. I shoot left-handed and felt like I needed to shift my swing radius a little.

The upstream turkey shut up, but the other one was still slowly coming, gobbling every 20 to 30 seconds. When I saw him he was 75 yards out. He advanced another 10 and stalled, still gobbling but not moving forward anymore. *Wish I had a decoy,* I thought. *He's waiting for the hen to show herself.*

Even with the gobbler in sight, the dense cover of my blind allowed me to pick up my box call and cluck at him. When I did, the upstream gobbler – the one who'd been eluding me, the one who had shut up on me, the one I'd come there to kill – gobbled. He was directly behind the wide trunk of my tree. He couldn't have been more than 10 feet away – yes, feet – but he was as safe from me right then as if I'd been sitting there with a slingshot and a pocket full of Chinaberries.

This turkey had just re-taught me one of turkey hunting's basic axioms, to wit: Being able to cover multiple approaches doesn't do a hunter much good if he doesn't then pay attention and cover them. The uphill gobbler had taken advantage of my single-minded focus on his downhill buddy and made his way to the one 20-degree sliver of my surroundings I couldn't see.

I felt foolish for letting it happen, but it wasn't a new feeling. Anyway, no big. There was still that downhill gobbler out front, and I felt sure he'd come to the bird behind me. All I needed to do was be still and wait. So I calmed down a bit, took a breath and looked out front again to find the downstream gobbler. To borrow a punchline from an old Sven and Ole joke: "*…and dere he vas…GONE!*"

Vere he vent…um, excuse me…where he went, I have no idea. Nor do I know why he went there. All I can say for sure is I never saw or heard him again. So there I was, pinned down like a butterfly in a high school sophomore's bug collection. The turkey I'd been hunting for most of a week was almost close enough to pet, and there wasn't one blessed thing I could do about it. I knew he was still there because now he was drumming and dragging his wings through the leaves.

This situation lasted for, oh, I don't know. A month, maybe. He never gobbled again, but the drumming and leaf-raking was nonstop. Until, between one minute and the next, it wasn't there anymore. I was cutting my eyes from one side to the other, trying to catch sight of him coming around my tree, but he never did. After another month or so I risked leaning out and peering behind me.

And dere he vas, also…GONE!

Chapter 7

The Eight-Hour Gobbler

It had been a quiet opening morning. Nothing answered the crows and owls at dawn, and nothing answered my walking and calling over the three hours that followed. It was a little after nine when I heard him gobbling at a mob of crows that were evidently trying to peck his head off. The turkey was making a lot of racket, but he was a long way off across a deep, steep-sided hollow. The whole valley was a three-year-old clearcut, and a dense thicket of vines, brambles and hardwood saplings now covered the leftover ground slash. Crossing that mess was going to be time-consuming, difficult and painful.

But this was 30 years and 40 pounds ago, and this bird was the only one I'd heard all morning. He was gobbling good even if it was at crows, and after all, it was Opening Day. I was rested and fresh. I debated the pros and cons of going after him, but you already know how that worked out.

It took me nearly an hour to fight my way across the hollow. More than once, usually when I was picking myself back up after tripping over a limb or rock hidden in blackberry canes, I wished I'd never heard him in the first place.

But he was still racking 'em off pretty good when I topped the far slope, bleeding and sweating, and stepped into the blessedly open and briar-free woods with the turkey. He was 200 yards out there, maybe a few yards closer. At any rate, far enough for me to gain some ground on him, take time to select a good set-up spot about 150 yards from the gobbler, and stick a green bush or two in front of my tree before calling. As I scrooched around to get comfortable before letting the gobbler know I was there, I glanced at my watch. Ten o'clock.

He cut off my first run of yelps. *All right,* I thought. *This won't take long.* Famous last words. I set the battered old box call in the leaves, stuck a triple-reed cutter in my mouth and shouldered my gun. I'd killed a bird here a few years before and had a pretty good handle on how the place laid out. There was nothing but flat, open, mature woods between the turkey and me.

Eighty minutes and God only knows how many gobbles later, the turkey wasn't an inch closer. He answered box, slate, diaphragm, and every crow that cawed within hearing distance. When the crows and I weren't calling, he answered his own gobbling. He was the noisiest turkey I'd ever heard, and in the three decades since I don't think I've heard his equal.

But, of course, you can't shoot noise.

At 11:30 I quit calling. He didn't. More time passed. So did another couple hundred gobbles. Somewhere around noon, another gobbler joined my bird and they gobbled back and forth for a while, adding to the racket. My ears were starting to hurt. So was my butt; that comfortable 10 a.m. set-up wasn't quite as comfortable at 1 p.m.

At that point I decided it was safe to stand up, stretch and pee. I dug out an apple and ate it. Drank some water. Walked a circle around my tree. Meanwhile, the turkey gobbled 30 times.

It was way, way past time to move. I closed the distance slightly when I did, but mostly I just flanked the turkey by moving 60 yards to my right to change the direction of my calling. The new set-up also gave the gobbler the option to approach me along an old but well-defined logging trace.

No surprise, he gobbled at my first call from the new spot. The second gobbler did not, and that gave me false hope. I thought the second bird might have gone silent and was sneaking in. I got vigilant. It went for naught.

By 2 p.m., it was obvious neither gobbler was coming in on the old trace road, or from any other direction. He was beginning to wind down in the frequency of his gobbling, but he was still racking one off every minute or two. Time to make another move. I continued my right-hand flanking maneuver, circling 100 yards this time until I was at the edge of the flat the turkey and I had been sharing for the past four hours. I set up with my back to the drop-off, but close enough I could see down the gentle slope in case the turkey decided to circle me and come in from below.

Not to worry. 3 p.m. came and went, and the turkey had neither moved nor stopped gobbling. I moved farther along the drop-off and made another set. Same sad story.

At 4 o'clock, I yelped and cut one last time, got the inevitable gobble in return, and then I ducked below the lip of the drop-off and ran 40 yards back toward my original set-up. I stuck my head up above the drop-off, yelped and ducked back down. I ran another 40 yards and repeated the process, then did the same thing three more times. Then I turned around and ran back 50 yards, slipped to the top of the drop-off and set up where I could cover both the flat and the slope.

Before I got settled in I could tell he was coming. And he came fast. I barely had time to get my mask up when I saw him, trying to strut and run at the same time. It would have been comical if I still had any sense of perspective about this hunt, but I'd lost that some time ago. He came by me too fast and too far out to risk a shot, and he was almost out of sight chasing the retreating hen when I clucked at him and he stopped. Ninety yards.

Then, unbelievably, he stalked right back the way he'd come, passing me this time plenty slow enough to shoot but 15 yards too far. I clucked at him again but he ignored it. For the first time since nine

The Eight-Hour Gobbler had reinforcements for a while, but apparently the other gobbler came to his senses after a while and went on his way before he burned out his gobble box.

a.m. he wasn't gobbling.

I waited 10 minutes after he was out of sight, and he didn't gobble. But when I yelped he answered me fast and eager. As near as I could tell, he was back at the same spot he'd been gobbling from all day. I moved back to one of my old set-ups and got him fired up again, but it was, as Yogi Berra said "déjà vu, all over again."

I gave up on the gabby gobbler at 5 o'clock, eight hours after I'd located him and seven after I'd started working him. Or since I started being worked by him, however you want to look at it. Either way, I'd had all I wanted of this damn turkey.

Yogi also said, "It ain't over 'til it's over." For me, though, this Opening Day was over. One more time I called, one more time he answered, one more time I gathered up my equipment and stood up.

As I took the first few steps back in the direction of that godawful clearcut that lay between me and my truck, he gobbled again.

"Shut up, turkey!"

He gobbled.

Chapter 8

Davy

If I'd been home, I'd have ignored the alarm clock, stuck my head under the pillow and gone back to sleep. It had started raining at ten p.m., it was pouring at two when Mother Nature called, and when the clock told me to get up at four it was still coming down hard.

But this was the first day of a three-week trip to eastern Tennessee, Kentucky and Ohio, and when you're on a turkey safari there's no such thing as taking a day off. You don't have to like it, but you still have to go. My thoughts were black and bitter as the so-called coffee they insult you with in cheap motels, and drinking a mug of the stuff while driving through the dark in a steady downpour didn't do a thing to improve my mood.

I hadn't had time to hunt when I reached Greenville the previous afternoon, but I'd map-scouted the nearby Cherokee National Forest and found a ridge that looked promising on both my topo maps and the satellite imagery on my mapping program. I drove out there just before sundown to put eyeballs on the place, figure out where to park and gauge how long the morning drive would take.

The only problem was the low water creek crossing between me and my spot. It had rained three inches during the night, and yesterday's trickle across the concrete slab was now a raging four-foot flood. A giraffe might have crossed it, but not a Dodge truck. I was only half a mile from where I wanted to park, but it might as well have been half a hundred.

There was a similar ridge on my side of the creek, so I backtracked a mile and pulled off the road where the topo map hinted the climb might be easiest. Meanwhile the rain slacked off considerably, and by gobbling time it quit. I looked up the steep slope. Maybe it was the easiest route, but it still wouldn't be a stroll in the park, especially with everything wet and slippery. I was going to need both hands and both feet to get up there.

I was listening to the *drip-drip-drip* of the recently drenched forest and feeling pretty wishy-washy about the whole affair when a turkey gobbled up on top. No more wishy-washy. I grabbed my gun and vest, stuck my old Lohman box call into a Wonder Bread sack, and headed uphill. In those few seconds, he gobbled three more times. He sounded angry, and that gave me hope. I like hunting angry turkeys; they make mistakes.

He had worked himself into a fizz by the time I slipped and pulled and crawled and floundered my way upward. I came to the top about 150 yards west of him, and as near as I could tell he was roosted in a clump of over-mature eastern white pines just off the south side of the ridge.

This was an inhospitable spot in which to hunt a turkey. The angle of the slope near the top was even steeper than it had been 800 vertical feet below – something approaching 30 degrees. That doesn't sound like much on paper, but it's pretty steep when you're standing on it.

The vegetation up here was sparse and low, with big chunk rock scattered around thick enough to make groundline sight distance a serious concern. Even if I was able to call him to me through this stuff, I knew he'd use the rocks to his advantage and would be right in my face before I saw him.

There were positives, though. First, the top of the ridge was intermittently cloaked in swirling, misty fog, and the ground litter was soft and silent from the nightlong rain. By timing my approach to coincide with the foggy moments, I was able to get much closer than normal before setting up. Second, the turkey was still in the tree, and he was roosted far enough off the razorback spine of the ridge I figured he'd fly down on my side.

Another thing working in my favor, or so I thought, was that his roost tree was almost on the end of the ridge, with no more than 50 feet of ground between the trees and a bluffy slope that dropped almost vertically toward the creek I hadn't been able to cross. It didn't leave him much of a landing zone in that direction, so I figured the odds were good he'd pitch out my way.

And a final bit of luck, I found the perfect set-up spot less than 75 yards from the pines – a vertical boulder wider than my shoulders and taller than my head, with a smaller, perfectly level rock in front of it that made the perfect seat. With my seat cushion, it was as comfortable as a high-end movie theater chair and I was looking directly at the pines. All I needed was popcorn and a Coke.

It didn't work out, of course. After all, this book is titled B*ad Birds,* not *Good Gobblers.* This particular bad bird kept gobbling every minute or so, and when the fog finally rose and the overcast started showing blue in places, I figured he'd soon come to the ground. But when another hour passed and he was still in the tree, I modified my game plan. Because of his position at the point of the ridge, I'd elected to stay quiet until he came down and not call even then if I didn't have to. I was confident he'd land within shotgun range. I didn't want to wait half the morning for him to do it, though, so I waited until he gobbled again and then hit him hard with a short but explosive cut/yelp sequence and got my gun on my knee.

That was the last time he gobbled that morning, and five minutes later he sailed off the end of the ridge and across the rain-swollen creek to the ridge I'd originally planned to hunt. Ten minutes later he started gobbling over there, as safe from me as if he'd been in Bangladesh.

I'd not heard another turkey gobble all morning, but I spent the rest of it moving west a mile on the south side of my steep ridge, crossing the top and working my way back east on the north slope. I got a turkey to answer me twice about 11:30 on the north slope, but the steep and rocky ridge made for slow going and by the time I got to his neighborhood I couldn't locate him.

*　　*　　*

The nice thing about headwater streams is, once the rain stops they return to normal almost as fast as they rose to flood stage. By early evening my little creek was down to about a foot of water going across the slab, and I crossed it easily. It was too late to climb the ridge (it was almost as steep as the one I'd already been on) but I did drive along the base of it at fly-up time and listen for gobbling. I heard three gobblers, spaced evenly along a mile of the ridge. One of them was close to the west end, and I figured he was the bird I'd messed with that morning.

The second morning dawned still and clear, and first light found me on top of the ridge 300 yards east of where I judged the gobbler would be roosted. My mood was considerably better this second day.

I misjudged his roosting spot, but not badly enough to make a difference. He was 400 yards away, and between his first and third gobbles I cut that in half. This ridge was a lot more hunter-friendly than the one on the other side of the creek. It wasn't a razorback and instead had a narrow but flat top, varying in width from 50 to 80 yards. I set up 150 yards from the turkey. I could have gotten closer, but I was 30 yards east of one of the pinch points where the ridgetop was narrowest and had a good tree and good visibility. It was a good set-up.

I didn't hit the turkey as hard with my calling this morning, but I did give him a couple tree calls spaced two minutes apart. When he

66

jumped on the second one I laid the slate call in the leaves.

I was too far away to see him leave the tree, but I heard him when he did. Seconds later I saw him sailing straight at me. He landed almost within shotgun range, just beyond the pinch point. He gobbled as soon as his feet touched the ground, and somehow I resisted the urge to call. The woods were too open and he was too close; I figured calling under the circumstances would hang him up. He was interested. Let him look.

I hadn't planned on having competition, but when I heard the hen yelping behind me and the gobbler answered her, I figured I was a lucky man. She was some distance away, and even if she was coming to the gobbler I thought there'd be time for him to cover the 20 yards that would make him killable.

Nope. She evidently came at a trot, because the next thing I knew she yelped right behind me and walked by at 15 yards, bringing with her another hen. They approached the gobbler, passed him like they didn't even see him, and he turned and followed them off the side of the ridge. I tried to stop him but didn't have a chance and knew it. He went all the way to the road at the foot of the ridge, coming out about where I'd parked my truck. From there he went east, away from the creek, away from my truck, away from me. He was still gobbling when he went out of hearing.

It was still early morning and I could hear one of yesterday's gobblers a quarter mile down the ridge, so I went to him and set up. After a decent interval I called him in, but he turned out to be a precocious jake and I let him walk. I covered more of the ridge without any action, and then worked my way back to see if I could find the first gobbler. Sure enough, I found him. But he was far down the slope, still down there on the road, and he gobbled back at me several times but wasn't buying what I was selling. He probably still had the hens with him.

Because he was again pretty close to my truck, he sort of had me handcuffed. He wouldn't come to me, and I didn't want to spook him by going to the truck. So when he quit gobbling at high noon, I found a more comfortable tree, ate a snack and took a nap.

He woke me at 12:45 by gobbling in my face. I'm sure I jumped because when I got my eyes open good, he was running full speed and already almost out of range. Since I no longer shoot at running or flying turkeys, I didn't even raise my gun.

*   *   *

The third morning he didn't gobble on the roost and I thought maybe he'd moved back across the creek to the razorback ridge. But I didn't hear him over there either, so I stayed where I was. No sense chasing after something that might not be there. About 9:30 I heard him. I was on top and he was down on the road, 800 feet below me in altitude, 350 yards below me in distance. Again, he was close to my truck. I went downhill angling east, wanting to get on his level without being seen or heard. When I reached the road he hadn't gobbled for 15 minutes, but I hoped he was still close to where I'd heard him last. Easing to the last tree between me and the road, I peered around it like Kilroy peering over his wall, only my nose, eyes and forehead exposed.

He was 125 yards away, strutting within easy shotgun range of my truck. The bad part was, the truck was between us. I doubted I'd be able to call him past it, but this was the hand I'd dealt myself. Nothing to do but play it. I backed up the slope to the next suitable tree, set up and let out a long string of lost-call yelps on my raspy mouth call. I thought it sounded pretty good and so did the turkey. He answered with a hard, no-nonsense gobble, and I came right back with a short, snappy, *I'm-glad-I-found-you* set of four yelps. He gobbled at that, too.

Maybe this will work after all, I remember thinking. As has occasionally happened on other of my turkey hunts, I was wrong. Over the next 30 minutes I called to him three more times – once each with the diaphragm, with a box call and with a trumpet. He gobbled at each but held his ground. It seemed he was leery of the truck after all.

This wasn't a heavily traveled road, but it got some warm-weather traffic; it dead-ended two miles further east at a swimming hole on the creek that had flooded the road a few days before. This was a warm late-April day, and Saturday to boot. With each passing minute, the arrival of that dreaded next vehicle got one minute closer. I didn't know when it would happen, but I knew it was inevitable. Today? Tomorrow? I didn't know, but the clock was ticking.

Not relishing the prospect but having no other options, I climbed halfway back up the ridge and side-hilled nearly a quarter mile west, then came straight back down to the road almost at the low-water crossing. When I did the Kilroy thing again the gobbler was still strutting in the road, now 200 yards from me. This time, though, the truck was no longer between us. I chose a good tree slightly uphill as before, settled in, and switched to a slate.

He answered the first yelps, and when he gobbled again five minutes later he was noticeably closer. I waited a little bit and yelped again. He cut me off. Closer yet. I got my gun up, confident as a heron in a goldfish pond.

And that's when the inevitable happened. I first saw the gobbler at 60 yards. He was strutting down the road toward me, coming slow but coming. Seconds after I saw him, he slicked down and got about four feet tall. He stood there a long five seconds, then stepped unhurriedly off the south side of the road. I heard gravel crunching behind me, and I lowered both my gun and my head. In a few more seconds here they came – a late '80s Dodge truck, powder blue except for a white driver's side door. A man and woman occupied the cab. Three noisy, towheaded kids, a chocolate Lab and a nondescript brindle mutt flopped and twisted around in the truck bed, wrestling and squealing and barking amongst an assortment of blow-up rafts, lawn chairs, ice chests, colorful towels and pool noodles.

I couldn't fault this family for wanting to go to the creek on a fine spring Saturday, but boy did their timing suck. Or maybe it was my timing. Either way, the turkey was gone. I gave him another hour and called several more times, but I neither saw nor heard him again that day.

*   *   *

Sunday morning, I gave this still unnamed turkey one last try. By now, it had soaked into my thick skull that this gobbler was telling me something: he liked that two-track road. So instead of driving across the low water crossing, I parked 200 yards west of it and walked across. Rather than climbing the ridge, I set up 20 yards south of the road, halfway between it and the creek, which paralleled the road downstream from the crossing. He started gobbling from his customary roosting area near the ridgetop, and I consider it one of the crowning accomplishments of my turkey hunting career that I resisted the urge to climb up there with him. (But maybe I'm breaking my arm patting myself on the back – maybe it was just because I'd climbed to him three days straight and was sick of it.)

He really put on a concert that morning, gobbling well over a hundred times before flying down and then continuing to gobble as he moved away from me, going east down the top of the ridge before going silent an hour after flydown. Through it all I sat there, growing more antsy by the minute but determined to stick with my game plan.

I was still sticking with it at 10 a.m. During that time, I'd seen two single hens and a tight, quarrelsome trio of jakes walk the road. Also three does and that same mostly blue truck full of kids, dogs and swim toys. I'd lost faith in my game plan, but if turkey hunting has taught me anything, it's the value of patience. At about 10:30, he gobbled. He was down the road toward the swimming hole, but I couldn't see him. I wanted to call but managed not to do it. Five minutes later he gobbled again, and he'd cut the distance some. I guesstimated he was still 150 yards away.

He gobbled again five minutes later and rattled the leaves. *Where was he???* I should have been able to see him. I was frantically scanning the road back and forth, back and forth. Nothing. He gobbled again, and I discovered the awful truth. He wasn't on the road like I'd thought. He was directly behind me, coming up the creek bank, and because I was less than 20 yards from the creek myself, he had to be closer than that.

My tree was wide enough to hide me from behind, but that wasn't going to be the case much longer. My only play was to lower my gun, switch from left to right shoulder, and bring the barrels around down low while I slowly twisted my upper body around to the left. Then I slowly brought the gun to my right shoulder and aimed at the creek bank with the barrels hard against the bark of my tree.

This maneuver took a full minute, maybe longer. While I was doing it, I heard nothing from the turkey, which told me nothing. Did he see me or hear me when I made the move? Did I spook him? Was he still back there? I could hold this awkward position for a few minutes, maybe, but I was in a serious bind and wasn't going to be able to stick with it very long.

He gobbled again. He was still behind me, but since I was twisted so far around my tree my front was now my back. He was on the road. Evidently, while I was making my turn to the left he made a turn to the right and walked by me. But now the advantage was mine. I was in very heavy shade and the gobbler was in full midday sunlight. As slowly as I could, I twisted back to a normal position. Midway through the move I picked up the turkey in my peripheral vision. He was in strut, facing the other way, and I got the gun on him before he turned. I wanted to wait and enjoy the moment, but I was still shooting wrong-handed with no arm support. I was already a little shaky.

When I clucked, his head came up over his fan like a jack in the box. I wasted no time doing my part. He was a good bird, not heavy but otherwise very well endowed. His spurs were sharp and curved, his beard was a rope.

Heading back to Greeneville, I was running possible names for this old warrior through my head. I'd been pondering it for two days, but nothing had grabbed me yet. When I came through the little community of Limestone I saw the sign pointing the way to Davy Crockett's birthplace.

Why not?

Davy wasn't heavy, but he was otherwise well endowed.

Chapter 9

The Firebreak Gobbler

There are places from which sane hunters would rather not hear a turkey. This was one of them. Not that it was a poor listening spot. Quite the opposite; it was a wonderful listening spot. It was only 150 yards from a well-traveled gravel road, it had a comfortable boulder as big as a sofa to sit on or lean against while you listened, and it overlooked a large section of mature forest that harbored a healthy turkey population.

The problem arose only if you heard a turkey gobble. The listening spot was a promontory that towered above a deep, wide, bowl-shaped valley, and the only way to get into that valley from way up there at the listening spot was to descend more than 200 yards through a rockslide of grapefruit- to ice chest-sized granite rocks. It wasn't a loose rockslide, exactly, although here and there a rock would move when you stepped on it. It was just tricky and time-consuming to find good footing, and going down through it required every bit of your attention. Coming back up was even worse.

But I was younger, stronger and dumber in 1983 than I am today, and I'd been hearing this bird gobbling down in there for two weeks before the season opener. I'd been hearing several, actually, but one was more consistent and more talkative than the rest. He was the turkey I wanted.

He favored a spur ridge thar ran east from the bottom of the rockslide. Five of the six pre-season mornings I'd listened, he'd roosted on that ridge. He may have been there the sixth morning, too, but nobody gobbled that day so I don't know.

From the listening spot I could tell there had been some bulldozer work done along the spine of the ridge. I suspected it was a firebreak, plowed in preparation for a controlled burn. I was proved right when I went in to listen one last time the day before the season opened. On the left side of the ridge – the north side – the woods had been burned, probably the day before, two days earlier at most. From my eagle's-eye view, it looked like a well-executed burn, good ground coverage, not too hot, and maybe a thousand acres in the total burn. There were still a few flames flickering here and there and quite a bit of smoke was still rising from smoldering logs and stumps. It swirled over the blackened ground like fog.

I'd killed a few turkeys by 1983, but I mean that literally: I'd killed a *few*. As in, three or four or five. To say I was still a greenhorn would be putting it mildly. I was so green I didn't know a fresh burn is a magnet to a wild turkey. Seeing all that smoke and ash devastated me. Here it was, the day before the season, I'd invested a week of spring sunrises patterning the roosting habits of this one turkey, and now some s.o.b. with a drip torch had wrecked my Opening Day game plan.

I felt that way for about ten seconds. That's how long I stood there, feeling like Frodo Baggins gazing out over the Desolation of Smaug, before my turkey gobbled from a pine tree out on the end of the ridge, 50 yards into the new blackness of the burn.

You could have knocked me over with a charred pine cone. Several other turkeys also cranked up in the few minutes following that opening gobble, but they barely even registered. I was locked onto the gobbler in the burn.

He made me late for work that morning. I wanted to see what he did after flydown, so I made myself comfortable against the boulder and waited. He was in his usual gabby mood, and I kept count – *"two, three…forty, forty-one…ninety-four, ninety-five…"*. I don't remember the total number before he flew down, but it was a bunch. And he kept it up when he hit the ground. Not as frequently as when was in the tree, but plenty enough for me to keep track of him as he wandered through the burn, probably breakfasting on roasted acorns and crispy crickets.

*   *   *

I was pumped, and sleep was elusive that night. The next morning, I was off the high listening point, down through the rockslide and standing on the firebreak at the beginning of the ridge half an hour before first light. I was 300 yards from where the turkey had roosted yesterday, but two times during the seven days I'd been there to hear him wake up he'd roosted close to the start of the ridge. I didn't want to go past him or spook him.

In the gray of dawn, two other turkeys gobbled in the distance, and that prompted the firebreak bird to tune up. When he gobbled he wasn't 50 yards away, perched right above the firebreak. I'd have bumped him if I'd gone any farther. Even back then I occasionally made a smart move.

I was close enough. Too close, really, but I didn't have enough savvy to know it. There was an oak tree at my shoulder that would give me a good view down the bulldozer scar, and after I slipped back and stuck a lone hen decoy 25 yards behind my set, I made myself comfortable beside that tree.

I have already told you I was green as a June cantaloupe. As soon as I got settled against my oak tree I stuck a mouth call in and cackled at his next gobble. (Cutting was an unplumbed art form for me in those days; I'd never even heard the term, and I'm not sure anybody else knew about it either.) He gobbled again. I cackled again. He gobbled. I cackled. Etcetera, etcetera. No tree yelps. No sleepy clucks. None of that soft, sissy stuff. Make his ears bleed, that was my game plan.

I hung him up in the tree, of course. He didn't leave the limb until nearly an hour past official sunrise. Thinking back, as close as he was and as much and as loud as I called, I'm surprised he flew down at all. To the best of my recollection, I didn't let a single gobble go unanswered.

When he did fly down, it surprised the dickens out of my greenhorn self that he flew down in the opposite direction. Of *course* he did, considering the abominable racket I'd been making for the past hour. He didn't go far, though, and I could see him standing in the firebreak looking back at my decoy. He gobbled at it, then strutted experimentally and gobbled again. Ol' Greenhorn cackled at both gobbles. Of *course* he did.

Unbelievably, the gobbler started back toward me anyway, strutting intermittently, slowly advancing along the smooth scar of the firebreak. He came back almost even with his roost tree, and I was going to give him another ten yards before killing him. But he turned to his left short of my mark and went into the unburned woods on the south side of the firebreak.

I was wondering what to do, and so I naturally did the wrong thing: I continued watching the open scar of the firebreak to the exclusion of everywhere else. I was like the drunk in the old joke who lost a quarter in the dark alley but was looking for it under the street light because he could see a lot better there.

When the turkey gobbled again he was 25 yards behind me, and I spooked him when I turned my head to look. He was standing right beside the decoy. He putted, ran down the firebreak and disappeared.

*   *   *

I went to him the next two mornings. The first day of the two, he was roosted at the end of the ridge. I overcalled to him again, and this time he flew all the way to the valley floor when he pitched out. For the first time since I'd met him, he didn't gobble after he hit the ground.

The third day of the season, he also didn't gobble on the roost. Nor did anybody else, at least not close enough for me to hear. With no other turkey to go to, I picked a good tree along the firebreak and stuck a leafy blind on the unburned side and settled in, determined to sit there all day.

His gobble woke me up at 10:25, but I didn't know where or how far. He gobbled again a couple minutes later, and this time I was awake enough to course the sound. He was 75 yards into the burn, straight ahead but out of sight below the slope of the ridge. I was working up enough saliva to yelp at him when I thought better of it. *Let's wait and see,* I remember thinking, and maybe the reason I remember it four decades later is because it was probably the first intelligent decision I ever made as a turkey hunter.

But my next decision wasn't quite as smart. I kept looking at the same spot where I'd coursed the sound, expecting him to pop up right there. (Slow study, me.) But he didn't. Duh. My laser-like focus was straight ahead, probably no wider than 10 to 15 degrees either side of my gun barrel, so it still surprises me that I saw him at all. He walked out of the burn onto the firebreak about 45 yards to my left – my wrong side.

If he'd been heading my way I could have just waited for him to walk in front of the gun, but he crossed the firebreak and walked into the unburned woods with me. Every step was taking him farther and farther into my wrong-shoulder zone, and even Ol' Greenhorn knew better than to move body and gun that far with him so close. So I clucked at him with the diaphragm, and he stopped, gobbled, and pulled himself into a strut. He didn't come closer, but he didn't keep moving to my left, either. He stood there drumming at me for what seemed like an hour. After that two-minute interval, he started walking again, and though he gobbled at my second cluck, he didn't stop. I had my head cranked around as far as it would go and my eyeballs cranked as far as they'd go, too, but he got out of sight and for a while I could hear the leaves crunching as he walked. But it got fainter, and pretty soon I couldn't hear it any more. I waited for what seemed like another hour, and after that two minutes had passed I leaned around my tree. No turkey.

*   *   *

I hunted him the next day. He didn't gobble.

I rested him a day, then hunted him again. He didn't gobble. Didn't gobble the next day, either.

I never hunted that turkey again. Even Ol' Greenhorn had enough sense to know when he was in a no-hope situation.

My wife says the reason turkeys disappear like that is because they go into turkey caves. But I didn't meet Jill until about 15 turkey seasons after all this happened, so I was still in the dark about that little-known piece of turkey lore. It has provided me with a ready-made excuse many times in the 25 years we've been hunting partners, and I am hereby applying it retroactively, across four decades, to the Firebreak Gobbler.

Chapter 10

The Backbone's Devil

The paved road follows the crest of a ridge that forms a peninsula jutting three miles into a large Corps of Engineers lake. The top of the peninsula is private land sprinkled generously with high-end retirement and summer homes, but a wide band of Corps land borders the lakeshore all the way around the peninsula. It's open to hunting, and it used to be well-stocked with turkeys.

At one spot about halfway out the peninsula, the Corps land rises to the top of the ridge and provides access along a 50-foot strip of the road on both sides. My normal practice when I hunted the place was to park at the narrow access strip, listen from the road so I could hear both sides of the peninsula, and go whichever way I heard turkey music. If I didn't hear anything, I'd play eenie meenie miney moe and bail off the ridge either north or south, then circle the entire peninsula and come back to my starting point from the other direction.

Because of several out-of-state trips back-to-back, I hadn't had time to do any scouting. So this morning, Opening Day, I was going in blind. I stopped along the public strip and was getting my stuff out of the truck when the turkey gobbled.

I have a rule where unscouted turkeys are concerned: One gobble is no longer enough to get me headed that way. But the second and third gobbles followed within the minute, and I was still pulling my gear out of the truck when he gobbled the fourth, fifth and sixth times. Good. A hot Opening Day bird.

He was a long way off down the hill, so I hurried. But the closer I got, the more I didn't like the situation. By definition, a peninsula is surrounded by water on three sides, and when I got close enough to figure out the turkey was now above my level, I realized he was on the other side of a 100-yard-wide cove. It was public land over there, too, but to get to the turkey I'd have to hike more than a mile along my side of the cove, cross over, then hike that mile-plus down the other side of the cove to get back to the turkey. And then, worse news, I'd have to retrace that journey to get back to the truck, which was already a half-mile and 600 steep vertical feet behind me.

Naw. Not an option for this old man. There was a time, yeah, but that time ended several years ago. The turkey was only 200 yards away, though, and he was gobbling like there was no tomorrow. So before abandoning hope, I gave him the obligatory college try, setting up on my side of the water in a long-shot attempt to call him across. Don't laugh; it happens.

But not often, and it didn't happen this time, either. We jawed back and forth for a while, and I even got him close enough to the water's edge to catch a couple glimpses of him in the woods on his side. But he wasn't about to fly across, and after an hour we both knew it.

The positive side of the story, to that point, was that I hadn't heard any hunters on the turkey's side of the cove, and it was a big place. Walking over there was out of the question, but a 15-mile drive would get me to a public access point within a mile of the gobbler. I was at the truck by 7:30 and at my destination before eight. The parking area was empty, and I lost no time taking off turkeyward.

The turkey's peninsula was quite a bit larger than the one I'd left, and it had a sharp, narrow crest that earned it the common hill-country sobriquet of "The Devil's Backbone." I like the name but it's been overused; I have personally hunted five Devil's Backbones in four states, not counting the one I'm talking about here.

That's beside the point, of course, but this is my story, and random things like that sometimes pop into my head when I'm heading toward a turkey. The parking spot was at the highest point – the beginning, really, of the Devil's Backbone formation – and the first part of the hike was downhill and easy going. That easy going stuff ended at the first of the three draws I needed to cross to get to the turkey.

They weren't deep draws but all three were steep-sided, with loose rock slopes. Since I knew all three went all the way to the crest of the Backbone, my easiest path was a straight line. I gritted my teeth and did it. When I crossed the third ravine I was about done in, but I knew I was in the turkey's wheelhouse. My first exploratory yelps drew an immediate, eager response, and he wasn't far off and downslope a little. Good. No need to go any farther.

I sat down at the tree I'd selected before I called, readied myself, and called again. He answered, much closer, but he's gone uphill to my right instead of coming to me. He was now slightly above my position, with a good vantage point from which to peer down on me. Not so good anymore, but I still figured I could make it work. In order to see me, he'd have to come over a little rise and he'd be 30 yards off the gun when he did. Since I shoot left-handed, he was playing into my strength on gun positioning. I shifted slightly to cover his approach from above.

The next time he gobbled he was straight off my left shoulder, downhill again and about 120 degrees from where my barrels were pointing. Not so good anymore. I cut my eyeballs that way just in time to see him come into sight around a blowdown, 25 yards away and looking. I was in profile, probably skylighted, and he didn't spook but he didn't like what he saw. Too much movement was required for me to make a slowpoke gun barrel adjustment, so I did the next best thing and froze in place, hoping he'd go behind something big enough for me to make my move.

He did, but what he went behind was the blowdown he'd just cleared. The next time I saw him he was 80 yards away, across the steep ravine I'd crossed minutes ago, heading up toward the Backbone's spine. I watched him go and gave him ten minutes to put some distance between us. Then I angled away from his path in my own climb to the top. Once on the other side I dropped down a little, found a shady spot, ate a little turkey vest food and took a nap.

When I woke up it was 11:30, 90 minutes after I'd seen the gobbler. I moved on down the slope to an old logging trace that ran parallel to the Backbone, then turned east and moved slowly toward where I thought the gobbler had gone. I was right, and he answered my second set of yelps. He was on the road, maybe 200 yards away. I set up just off the trace, snugged into a convenient gap in a cluster of big chunk rock where I could see all three approaches – the old trace road, the downhill slope and the uphill slope. I had my gun pointing along the road, but since he'd come in from downhill last time, I paid the most attention to that approach.

So of course he came in from uphill. I waited well past what I considered a reasonable time, and when I yelped softly he gobbled hard, right off my right shoulder and no more than 20 yards across the narrow road. He was very killable, but I was handcuffed again: too much movement required for a slowpoke aim adjustment, and too close to try a quick-draw – which almost never works anyway. He gobbled again a minute later. Now he was behind me, still uphill from the road and now 50 yards away. Next time it was 100 yards, and I never heard him again that day. After an hour, I trudged back to the truck and conceded Opening Day to the Backbone's Devil.

*　　*　　*

While I'd been working the turkey that morning, I'd been hearing another turkey gobble farther out on the Backbone. Jill hadn't had any action, so we went together the next morning. This time we went by boat and listened from the water. We didn't hear anything from the second turkey farther out on the peninsula, but the Devil cranked up right on schedule, close to where he'd been yesterday. He was roosted just off a narrow bench about halfway up the slope of the Backbone. We used the trolling motor to move 300 yards down the cove so the gobbler would have the sun in his face if he came in, grabbed our gear and climbed. Jill sat on the upper lip of the bench, and I backed up 30 yards and sat on the lower lip. Jill was a little less than 100 yards from the Devil, who was still singing merrily from his tree.

He was still in that tree, gobbling every 30 seconds, well after fly-down time. I'd given him a tree yelp early on, and after he answered I hadn't called any more. Now I was wondering if I ought to give him a little more encouragement. I was reaching for my box call when the second turkey, who hadn't made a sound so far, gobbled behind us, maybe 75 yards away. I slowly looked over my right shoulder and scanned the woods carefully. Seeing nothing, I rolled to my right and assumed a prone position beside my tree – not the best shooting set-up, but a safer move than scooting around the tree with a turkey that close.

I had a triple-reed cutter in my mouth, but I figured this second bird was coming to the Devil's gobbling so I held off, not wanting to mess up the dynamic I thought was taking place. He'd show up eventually if the Devil kept gobbling.

And, naturally, this was when the Devil chose to leave his tree. He sailed the 100 yards to Jill and a little more, and when his feet hit the ground he was smack dab between us. Since I'd just turned around to cover the back door, both of us now had our backs to him. Jill could see him, but he was too close to me for her to shoot. And I was completely out of whatever play was about to unfold, unless the second turkey showed up before the Devil could pick me out.

Which didn't take long, seeing as he was only 15 yards away. I'm pretty sure he'd never seen the bottom of a turkey hunter's boots before, but he evidently didn't like 'em. He clucked sharply and left the bench going downhill, and when he was well away from danger he gobbled again. The second bird gobbled back, and the two of them got together down by the water's edge. They gobbled at each other a little bit and shut up. We gave them an hour to do something, calling occasionally but mostly just listening, but it was a wasted hour. We spent the rest of the morning prospecting from the boat, setting up in four or five places to do some blind calling, but we'd have been better off just going fishing.

Why in the world would this sight spook a 15-yard turkey? Maybe it was those lines of yellow dots Timberline puts on their boot soles. But don't those look sort of like berries?

*   *   *

Because I'd spooked this gobbler three times in two days, it seemed a good idea to give him a rest. I hunted elsewhere for three days – unsuccessfully – and then tried the Devil one last time before leaving home for another multiple-state road trip. I parked at the usual spot, on the high knob at the start of the Backbone formation. I was in good time, so I just sat in the truck for a few minutes with all the windows down, enjoying the morning and finishing my coffee.

When he gobbled, he was no more than 30 yards from me, straight out the truck window, and I spilled coffee all over myself. He was much too close for me to attempt opening the truck door. But I had to get out there somehow, and I needed to do it both quietly and quickly.

It had been a long, long time since I climbed out the window of a vehicle. I can't say that anymore. I climbed over the center console and somehow ooched my less-than-svelte body out the passenger window without breaking my neck, grabbed my stuff through the back passenger-side window and sneaked downhill on the blacktop, tiptoeing like a teenager coming home late. I went into the woods well downhill from the turkey, circled until I had him between me and the truck, then slowly eased up the back side of the knob until it began to flatten out. The turkey hadn't gobbled again, but I knew I was less than 75 yards from his tree.

Well, he heard me messing around at the truck, I said to myself. But even if he did hear me, I was in a good position to bushwhack him when he got relaxed enough to fly down. So I settled in, listening hard for any hint he was still with me. The hint came in the form of a swishing branch and the sound of wings carrying a heavy load. He sailed not straight at me but at a slight angle, and when his feet touched the ground he was 35 yards away. The gun was already on him, but I held off as long as I thought I could. I didn't want it to end that quick.

He was a half-mile from where I'd worked the Backbone's Devil earlier in the week, so I can't swear if he was the same turkey or not. But like I said earlier, this is my story, and I say he was. Either way, he felt good over my shoulder and it was a very short carry to the truck.

Chapter 11

Ol' 600

Maybe that's an unusual name for a Bad Bird. I'm too close to the subject matter to give an unbiased opinion. But let me tell you how he got it:

We'd driven a day and a half to hunt the abundant public land near a friend's house in the Midwest, a friend whose name you'd recognize if I mentioned it. When we arrived about 6 p.m., the turkey was gobbling less than a half-mile from our friend's front door, just across the road on Corps of Engineers land, maybe 400 yards away. It was actually three turkeys, but one of them was making the large majority of the noise. We figured we were listening to a dominant bird allowing his subordinates to gobble some, but at the same time reminding them who was boss.

We could have made a hunt that afternoon. They were certainly close enough. But we were tired and we had a week to hunt and it was a one-turkey state and it was getting on toward fly-up time and we had a few more excuses, too, I forget exactly what, but the bottom line is we were tired. So we leisurely unloaded our gear into our friend's house (he was off turkey hunting somewhere) and spent the last hour of daylight sitting in the yard and listening to the gabfest across the road.

The dominant bird split off from his two acolytes just before sunset. He moved upstream along a small creek that ran close against a hardwood ridge, still gobbling quite a bit, and the two subordinate birds went downstream. When they flew up, the lesser birds were 500 yards from the boss.

It was an encouraging development. Our plan was to get between them and hope they came back together the next morning. We got up a half-hour earlier than we really needed to, considering we were sleeping less than a quarter-mile from the turkeys. But we had to cross 200 yards of open ground to reach the woods along the creek, and we needed the cover of darkness to pull it off.

I hooted at the dominant gobbler from the front yard the next morning and he started gobbling in the dark. He never let up. We made the short walk across the open land, forded the creek without getting too wet, and closed in on the turkey. When we got in tight we still had to wait 20 minutes for enough light to find good places to sit.

We like to sit on the same tree when possible, or at least no more than six feet or so apart so we can communicate. We were shoulder to shoulder and the turkey was still hammering when she elbowed me and whispered, "Well, that was gobble number 200." She'd started counting his gobbles when we crossed the road, and that hadn't been 30 minutes ago. That's some impressive arithmetic right there.

Less than 15 minutes later: "That was 300."

About then, the turkey flew down. While Jill had been counting, I'd been thinking about how to work him when he hit the ground. He was red-hot, so I decided I would be, too. As soon as I knew his feet were on dirt, I hit him with an aggressive combination of yelps and rapid-fire cuts, using a slate and a diaphragm simultaneously.

He went crazy and I did a little counting of my own. He let loose a string of seven gobbles in what I swear could not have been more than five seconds. The last one, as he ran completely out of breath, was just a hoarse croak, like a toad. Jill gave me another elbow. "Quit it. I can't count that fast."

I elbowed her back. "You better quit counting and get your gun up. We're fixing to be looking at a turkey."

She did. When her gun was settled at knee and shoulder, she said, "That was 347, if you're interested."

I took her word for it and started counting, too. At 388 (so says my log book; my memory ain't *that* good,) I saw him coming along the creek bank, not moving as fast as he was gobbling but still making pretty good time. He was 75 yards out when he left the creek and headed uphill on the side of the ridge. I'd expected that – they like to look down on the calling when they get a chance – but it still wasn't a good thing. He had much better visibility from an elevated position. Which, naturally, was why he did it.

He side-hilled along the slope, coming closer, still gobbling every five to ten seconds, and when he was 35 yards away he went behind a tree. Jill made her move. But this was no rookie turkey, despite the frequency of his gobbling. He did that old peek-a-boo trick, that thing where the turkey apparently goes behind a tree but then stops and pulls his head and neck back and catches you moving. Sure enough, he caught Jill. But he didn't know what the movement was, so he froze. Jill froze too. For the first time since we left the front yard, he wasn't gobbling.

For the space of a minute, nothing moved. We desperately needed him to go back behind that tree. He did, and Jill fine-tuned her point of aim to kill him when he came out the other side. You know what happened there: he didn't come out. Instead he made a hard right and marched 30 yards farther up the slope, which put him 10 yards out of range when he showed himself again. He stood up there for another minute or two, looking suspiciously down into the bottom, and then he started gobbling again and moved along the ridge the way he'd been going, in the direction of his two underlings. They'd been gobbling all morning, too, just not as much as the one we were after.

When he reached them – they weren't far down the way –

there came the sounds of a brief fight, after which only one turkey was gobbling. We all know who.

He kept going, the gobbles getting fainter but no less frequent. We could have followed, but that's low-percentage at best, and it was still early and we had other good places to check. We were walking back to the house when Jill said, "He gobbled more than 600 times, you know." And that's how Bad Birds get named.

*   *   *

Jill killed a good gobbler at one of those other good places about 11 o'clock that morning. I heard her shoot – we were hunting parallel ridges on national forest land – and a half-minute later she hooted. That was our signal of success, and since nothing was happening on my ridge I walked quickly back to our meeting spot so I could watch my wife come toward me through the woods with a gobbler over her shoulder. If you haven't had that pleasure, I truly feel sorry for you.

Anyway…back to Ol' 600. Jill was now tagged out in this one-bird state, so we took the afternoon off and spent it windshield-checking several other nearby spots we'd found via map-scouting. Two of them looked highly promising, but that old bird-in-the-hand mindset had me by the throat. First light next morning found us already across the road, the open ground and the creek, waiting in the edge of the woods for that first gobble of many.

We'd listened to the evening serenade from the front yard, and we knew the three gobblers roosted pretty much where they had yesterday, and again we were between them. Ol' 600 cranked up first, and he was answered by the two gobblers behind us. We were pretty much in the middle, 200 yards or so from everybody. Good enough.

We set up on the same tree again, about 30 yards closer to Ol' 600 than we'd been yesterday. Today, though, our game plan was different. I gave him some soft tree calls early on, then shut up until he hit the ground. When he did, I again jumped all over him with the cutting/yelping gabfest, and while he was gobbling himself into cardiac arrest in response, Jill got up and scooted 50 yards back toward the subdominant gobblers downstream. I shut up and she took over the calling duties from her new position. 600 kept gobbling and she egged him on. When he started our way, she shut up too.

The theory was he'd come looking for the hen as he'd cone the day before, and I'd be up front to intercept him before he started uphill.

What he did, though, was cross the creek well upstream. Then he came down along the edge of the open ground, gobbling and looking, and he came by me out of range. Not far, but far enough. When it was apparent he was passing me by, I started calling to try to stop him. He ignored me, passed Jill too, and joined up with his servants downstream. After he delivered the morning ass-whipping, all three birds followed yesterday's route and passed out of hearing, still gobbling.

*   *   *

The next two mornings we tried those two good-looking areas we'd map-scouted. They didn't pan out. But we'd given 600 a couple days rest, and so the fifth morning of our hunt we went back to try him again. From the previous evening's gobbling activity, we knew he and his buddies were roosted in their customary places.

This time we went well downstream, even below where the two subordinate gobblers roosted. The creek was deeper and harder to cross, but we made it and found a good set-up along the travel route the gobblers favored after their morning meet-up. There followed one of the hardest hunts I've ever experienced as a turkey hunter. The plan was to not call at all, and simply ambush this son of a bitch when he came by.

That sounds easy, right? Just sitting there and listening? Try it

If you haven't had the pleasure of watching your wife come out of the woods with a gobbler in tow, you've missed one of the true pleasures of turkey hunting – and of life.

sometime when you've got a gobbler tearing the leaves off the trees and setting them on fire 450 yards away, and you have half a dozen calls within arm's reach. For the 90 minutes between his first gobble and the time one of his buddies popped up at 15 yards and screwed everything up, I was jittery as a convict at a parole hearing.

The gobbler seemed to like traveling up off the creek bottom, so we'd made our morning set 30 yards up the side of the ridge. Ol' 600 was being his usual gabby self, so there was no problem keeping up with his whereabouts. He gobbled his customary bezillion times on the roost, flew down, strolled by and picked up his buddies, whipped one or the other or both, and moseyed our way. At 100 yards, I saw all three of them. We already knew he was a big turkey, and I was expecting him to be noticeably bigger than his buds. But we had them in full view for five minutes and the only way we could distinguish 600 from the other two was the frequency of his gobbling. I decided I'd shoot whichever of the three offered me the first chance.

They were traveling close together, and at a range of about 60 yards they disappeared into a little dip on the side of the ridge, a dip we hadn't noticed when we made our set in the near-dark. I saw it after daylight, but the tree we were on was comfortable and offered a great field of fire with the exception of that one dip. I rolled the dice and we stayed put. It came up snake eyes.

Ol' 600 was in rare form that morning. After they dropped out of sight he kept us informed, and I had my gun on the sound as he came on, adjusting my aim with each new gobble. All he had to do was poke his head up at 15 to 20 yards and I'd uncap it for him.

But one of his subordinates was running interference, and he popped up about 30 degrees to the left (uphill) from all the gobbling. I knew it wasn't the turkey I was after, but I also knew I'd already made that decision.

There were two other things I knew about this situation. First, at 15 yards, it wasn't going to take this gobbler long to pick us out. Second, I wasn't going to be able to move my barrel through a 30-degree arc without getting busted. My only hope was for the dominant turkey to get there and show himself before his running buddy saw us and spooked.

He gobbled one more time before it all went sideways. The sound was a couple degrees right of my barrel, and the gobbler we had in sight saw me make that slight move. He clucked sharply, then started putting, rolled away from us and started running uphill, holding his head high. I jerked the gun back to my left and was going to shoot him in the back of the head, but he put a tree between us before I could get on him. I didn't see him again, and naturally Ol' 600 and the other turkey disappeared as well.

I killed a fat two-year-old two hours later on one of those good-looking places we'd hunted the day before. He was a fine turkey and he did what he was supposed to do, and I didn't make any unfixable mistakes and I killed him cleanly. I enjoyed the hunt. But as I carried him down toward the truck, I couldn't help but wish I had another tag.

*   *   *

We had a couple days before we had to be at our next hunt, so we slept in the next morning. When I opened the door at about 7 a.m., the first thing I heard was Ol' 600, belting 'em out at a rate of 10 gobbles a minute. He was still talking when we rolled out the driveway an hour later.

Chapter 12

The Coon Creek Sneak

It's one of the easiest places to find a roosted gobbler I've ever hunted. At the same time, it's one of the most frustrating places I've ever hunted. Gobblers can leave the roost in what are apparently dozens of ways, and I've never caught them doing it the same way two days in a row.

Picture a smallish tributary creek running generally east through a valley with equal amounts of open ground and hardwood timber. A county road crosses the creek, and two miles downstream the creek dumps into a sizable river. The land upstream, west of the bridge, is all pasture and all private. Everything between the bridge and the river is public.

South of the creek and east of the bridge, there's a pretty good hill. The locals call it a mountain, but it only rises 300 feet so it hardly qualifies. Still, it's rough and rocky and steep as a cow's face, and by the time you reach the top you understand the local "mountain" mindset.

North of the creek, the high ground isn't quite as high, rising only a hundred feet above the creek bottom. It's bluffy and broken, though, with vertical ledges, Volkswagen-sized boulders and an irregular canopy of big, over-mature oak, hickory and ash. The bluff runs the entire length of the creek between road and river, but it's cut into five sections by four wet-weather drainages that run from the high ground to the creek. Somewhere along this bluff is where the turkeys almost always roost, but two miles is a long way and though I can usually find them, I can't always get to them before they fly down.

That's why, when I hunt Coon Creek Bottom, I start my hunt in the low ground of the creek bottom rather than up on the bluff with the turkeys. I could probably hear better from the top of the bluff, but I can cover ground easier, quieter and much faster in the flat creek bottom, and that gives me a better chance of getting close while they're still in the trees.

There was a week left in my home season when I went to Coon Creek that spring. I'd been hunting out of state, and this would be my first hunt on "my" turf. To maximize my chances when I hunt this favored old honey hole, I always walk a half-mile from the bridge before gobbling time. I can hear all the way back to the bridge, and a half-mile farther east as well. First blush of dawn that morning found me at my customary listening spot, already cooled down from the brisk half-mile walk.

When the gobbling started, I could barely hear it. It was one gobbler, and he sounded like he was west of the bridge on the private land. But I knew better; there's nowhere for a turkey to roost in a hayfield. As it turned out, he was as close to the private land as he could get and still sleep in a tree. There was a huge pine at the edge of the county road right-of-way, and he was in it, looking down at the gravel roadway and my truck, parked less than 50 yards from his limb. I felt pretty smug when I saw the situation, figuring at worst I had a 50-50 chance of him flying my way. I backed off, climbed to his level and got as close as I dared. When I sat I was slightly uphill from him and 60 yards away.

I could see the grill of my truck and about 10 yards of the gravel road through a gap in the trees, and a decent interval after my normal tree yelp and the resulting return gobbling, he pitched out and landed smack in the middle of that 10-yard patch of gravel. If I'd been sitting in the passenger seat of my truck, I could have swatted him with a crappie pole.

He strutted there for a minute or so, oblivious to the truck, and when I yelped at him he spun to face me and gobbled hard. I called again and he came toward me until I couldn't see him any more under the road cut. But he never came up the embankment and into the woods with me, and when he gobbled again a couple minutes later he was in the creek bottom, downhill and south of me. When he gobbled a minute after that he was back in the road but behind my truck and out of sight, and the next time I heard him he was across the road in the private pasture, headed west away from where I could hunt him. He answered my calling as he left, but each answer was farther away and before long he was gone.

It was still early, so I went east toward the river, staying on the high ground this time, and before long I found another gobbler to play with. He made me work some, but I eventually found a stage he was willing to die on, and by nine o'clock I was back at the truck with a fat two-year-old over my shoulder.

I couldn't hunt that afternoon because of the one-a-day rule, but I did go back and listen for roosting birds at dusk. Heard one, too – a single gobbler, a quarter-mile east of the bridge. It was a popular roost spot, and I liked it because it was easy to get to from the road and I could get there quietly, in the dark, and set up at eye level with the turkeys roosted off the edge of the bluff in the big oak trees. When they roosted along this section of the bluff, they often simply pitched laterally and landed on the flat at the top of the bluff.

*   *   *

Which is exactly where I was sitting at first light. He gobbled on cue, at eye level and 40 yards away, but I couldn't see him because he was squarely behind the trunk of his tree. No, I wouldn't have limb-swatted him, but I would have enjoyed watching him gobble because he really put on a concert that morning.

Because he was so close, I was nervous about calling. Finally, though, after about his hundredth gobble, I made a few little peepy tree yelps. He didn't gobble, but I did get my first glimpse of him when he craned his neck and peered around the trunk of his roost tree. He pulled his head back, and a minute later I got my second glimpse as he set his wings and glided straight away, all the way across Coon Creek Bottom. He landed a third of the way up the "mountain" on the other side and set up shop. I left him gobbling there an hour later and went searching for another turkey. Found one, too, but he wasn't as amenable as yesterday's two-year-old, and when he left me at two p.m. I was on a bluff overlooking the river.

I'm not much of an afternoon turkey hunter, except *some* afternoons. Since it was well past midday and I was two hard miles from the truck, this appeared to be one of them. I ate a can of Viennas and a stick of string cheese and some crackers, then took a much-needed nap there on the river bluff.

At four p.m. I started working my way back along the roosting bluff, calling soft, moving slow. I crossed three of the four drainages and was halfway through the fourth section of the bluff when, not far from where the morning's gobbler had flown away, a turkey gobbled. On his own, mind you, not in response to crow or hawk or woodpecker or me. A good omen. He wasn't far ahead of me, and I sat immediately. I waited five minutes to see if he'd give me another gobble and maybe provide some information. I was drawing in air to yelp to him on a diaphragm when he gobbled from the same place, and I changed my mind about the yelp and cut at him instead, quick and explosive. He double-gobbled, and though I couldn't recall how it got there, my shotgun was suddenly at my shoulder and pointing downrange. My breath came short in my chest.

Nothing happened for one minute. Nor two. Nor five, nor

ten, nor fifteen. I was debating whether to call again when the turkey gobbled, way too close for comfort. There was a problem, though. He was behind me.

Excuse me. There were two problems. The second one was, when he gobbled over my shoulder, I'd flinched like a mule getting bit by a horsefly. Now, having a turkey gobble directly behind you isn't good, but it's not always an insurmountable problem. Flinching violently when he does it, however, almost invariably is. An insurmountable problem, I mean. My flinch was followed immediately by a sharp *putt!* And then the sound of a two-legged animal running rapidly through dry leaves.

* * *

The next morning, my third day in pursuit of the Coon Creek Sneak, he was roosted 300 yards east of the site of yesterday afternoon's debacle. This time I set up below him, against a maple tree in a little open grove of maples and boxelders in the creek bottom. I figured it was about time he pitched down into the bottom from the roost. Coon Creek turkeys do that sometimes, and he hadn't done it yet.

He didn't do it this day, either. After he flew down onto the flat ground at the top of the bluff, I waited until I could tell if he was moving or not (he was, slowly, toward the river.) Soon as I figured that out, I took off at a fast walk through the bottom, wanting to get ahead of him before he reached the next drainage cut. I beat him to the cut by a couple hundred yards and hustled up the rocky bed of the drainage until it petered out on the flat, where I made a hurried set against a fallen log and waited. I was going to bushwhack this sorry thing and make up the biggest whopper you ever heard.

But for reasons known only to the gobbler, he angled downhill just before he reached the cut and went across it just above where it flattened out in the creek bottom. I saw him go by me at 80 yards, and there was nothing I could do about it but watch. When he got to the

I'd been mistaken. The fifth day was a lot better.

run of the drain, he followed it to the creek and that's where I lost sight of him.

* * *

On the fourth day he didn't gobble from the roosting bluff. He didn't gobble from anywhere, nor did any other gobbler within my range of hearing. It was one of those Silent Spring mornings Rachel Carson warned us about so long ago; not even the cardinals were singing. No warblers, titmice, or dickeybirds of any kind. Even the crows didn't have much to say, and I hunted until 12 straight up and never heard the first turkey sound.

* * *

The fifth day wasn't much better. I did hear him gobble four times from far east along the roosting bluff, but by the time I got to him he was on the ground. He gobbled once more, then struck out north away from Coon Creek, and the last time I heard him he was near the public land boundary and evidently headed for the dairy farm across the fence.

Having nothing else to do, I stayed in the vicinity of that last gobble for the rest of the morning, moving my set-up a little bit from time to time, calling softly. You know, just trying to sound like a bored hen turkey. It was closer to one o'clock than to twelve, and I told myself I'd make one more change and then call it a day. I moved 40 yards north, which brought me within view of a pasture on the dairy farm, and before I could get settled in and make a call, the turkey gobbled from the edge of the pasture. I clucked a single time, raised my gun, and killed him at 35 yards as soon as he finished snaking underneath the lowest strand of barbed wire.

I'd been mistaken. The fifth day was a *lot* better.

Chapter 13

The Ankle Bracelet Gobbler

My pre-hunt research failed me. I'd hunted Maine before, and this time wanted to get farther north, where the small private acreages thinned and the big, open-to-the-public timber company holdings grew. Turkeys had advanced steadily north during the intervening five or six years, and I wanted to hunt them in their new stomping grounds.

It was a good plan but for one thing: In my zeal to get north of the small properties, I also got north of most of the turkeys. We did find sign in most places we looked, but not much, and in a day and a half of hard, diligent hunting/scouting, we never heard or saw a single turkey.

It was looking like Randy and I had made the 1700-mile drive from Arkansas for nothing. But there we were, and we were determined to make the best of it. That's why the second day's noon found us driving circles around a good-sized public area, consulting maps, online hunting apps and dead reckoning in a futile effort to find access to the place.

Then we bumped into a wildlife officer, and after the obligatory license check he rained on our parade by telling us the area we were trying to get to was pretty low on turkeys.

"But look," he said, borrowing my phone and dropping a pin

on my OnX. "There are several fields surrounded by woods along this road here. See 'em? Here's a good one, and I've been seeing birds in this field, too." He pointed to several fields near the pin, scattered through an otherwise heavily wooded area of about a thousand acres under sole ownership. "They're hay fields, and I know the owner. He won't be cutting for another three weeks, and he lets anyone hunt, but I don't think anybody's been there for two weeks. We don't hunt turkeys much this far north."

In turkey hunting, nothing comes that easy. But this new place wasn't far, and we quickly headed that way. When we drove into the first field, we ran a gobbler and two hens out of it. Second field: two gobblers and three hens. Slow learners, us Arkies.

At the third field, we parked well back down the narrow access lane, suited up, and eased slowly to the edge of the field, glassing carefully as things came into view. Nothing was there, of course. You know how that stuff goes. But both the access road and the field edge showed plenty of sign, both fresh and old.

*   *   *

Next morning, we misjudged the length of the drive from town, or were too slow getting ready, or something, because it was well past turkey wake-up time when we reached the area. Nothing was gobbling anywhere. Randy dropped me off near my field and drove two miles south to his. Nothing was in the field, and I took off into the woods.

Nothing happened for a while, but about nine o'clock I heard a faint gobble back in the direction of the field. Five minutes later he gobbled again.

Even on a slow morning, one distant gobble won't pull me. Two gobbles usually will. He gobbled twice more while I closed on him, and sure enough, he was in the field when I got there. It wasn't a big field, maybe 10 acres, but he was smack in the middle of it, shepherding three hens. It was a low-percentage play, but I'd been covering ground for more than four hours (dawn comes early in central Maine) and here was this gobbler, see? I crawled through the knee-high grass to a big pine near the edge of the field, on a little point that stuck a few yards into the open.

My set was shady when I made it at 9:20, but by 11:45, that had changed. The weeds hid me well enough from the turkeys, but knee-high weeds provide decidedly inferior shade. Even in Maine, the late-May noonday sun is hot when you can't hide from it.

Trouble was, the gobbler would answer almost everything I threw at him. And trust me, in the 2-1/2 hours I'd been fooling with him, I went through every pitch I knew and made up a few more on the spot.

Gobble he would. Come he would not. When Randy sent me a 1 p.m. text saying he'd had no action, we called it a day. I back-crawled into the heavier cover, stretched, and started to leave. But first I sent one last, rude cut-cackle sequence fieldward. The longbeard rewarded me with a lusty triple-gobble, and he answered that old Lohman box until I was out of hearing.

*   *   *

We got there earlier the next morning, but it still wasn't early enough. Dawn comes earlier and stretches out longer in central Maine than in central Arkansas, and we hadn't yet learned to deal with it. Same as yesterday, nobody was gobbling. Randy dropped me off and I took a calculated risk by cutting across a corner of my field, hoping the gobbler wasn't roosted where he could see me.

But he was. I was almost to my previously chosen set-up tree when he busted out of an eastern white pine less than 100 yards away. I watched him disappear into the growing dawn, then threw my hat into the wet grass and stomped on it.

107

I said several mean things to myself as I picked up my hat and trudged the remaining few yards to my tree, but in the back of my mind I was thinking this greenhorn miscue might be a blessing in disguise. The gobbler was now separated from his hens. But I was still muttering self-insults when, 30 minutes later, he gobbled way over there toward the rising sun. I knew there was a much smaller field over that way, and it sounded like he was close to it. Off I went.

He wasn't in the field but he was close, in an open patch of mixed hardwoods. He left me enough room to get between him and the field, which also put the rising sun behind me. He gobbled hard into the back of my first run of yelps, and three minutes later I saw him coming at 90 yards. He was 60 yards out when a hen came past my left shoulder almost close enough to touch.

I reacted fast, taking my trigger hand off the gun (I shoot lefty) and making a quick jerky motion at the hen. She blew into the air with a panicky-sounding cackle and the longbeard slicked down. He didn't spook, but he was suspicious. He stood still as a telephone pole much longer than I wanted to sit there with my gun to my shoulder, and after what seemed like an hour but was probably 5 to 10 minutes, he loosened up, shook himself like he'd just finished a dust bath, and walked off in the direction the hen had flown. I clucked and purred at him as he walked away, but there was nothing for it. He'd lost confidence in my set-up spot, and that was that. I got back on him later in the morning and he gave me hope for about 90 minutes, but in the end it was another goose-egg for both members of the home team.

*   *   *

The third day, we finally made it to the area in decent time. We might as well have slept in, though, because it was well past 7 before I heard the first gobble. He was back in Randy's direction and a long way off, but I knew Randy was two miles from me and was almost certainly too far away to hear him. There was a field between us and neither of us had hunted it. As I approached it, it became apparent that the gobbler was in that field. Oh goody, I'd had such good luck with field turkeys on this trip.

He'd gobbled a lot during my long approach, and when I got closer I figured out why: he was being worked by another hunter. I knew it wasn't Randy because the guy was using a wingbone or trumpet, so I sat down against a comfortable tree to listen to the hunt play out. It wasn't like I had any other gobbling turkeys to chase after.

At first, it sounded at first like the hunter was going to win, and I was surprised to find myself rooting for him. The gobbler answered his every call, and the guy was playing it conservatively; he had a hot gobbler and knew it, and seemed content to wait and not force the play. The gobbles got closer and closer to the wingbone, but then they started getting noticeably farther away, in the direction of a power line right-of-way that ran across the west end of the field I'd been hunting.

The wingbone calling stopped, and I figured the hunter was repositioning somewhere close to the power line. But then I heard the unmistakable sound of a muffled dirt bike coming to life, and the sound receded in the opposite direction the gobbler was going. Twenty minutes later the gobbler had reached the power line and was headed north. He wasn't gobbling as much as before, but it was enough for me to keep track of him. I was back in the game.

I took off through the woods on a parallel course, forced-marching through the thick woods. I got even with him, then a little ahead. I hustled on another 200 yards and angled over to the right-of-way. I was at the edge, looking for a suitable set-up, when he gobbled 75 yards away. He was in the right-of-way, but fortunately there was a lot of cover between us.

Fortunately in one way, that is. He couldn't see me, but that was a two-way street, and he'd be hidden until he was right on top of me. I was trapped, with no set-up tree anywhere close. I did the only thing available to me: sat down with no backing behind a bushy northern white cedar. At least I was in deep shade – which, probably, was the only thing that saved me.

I shifted the triple-reed diaphragm from cheek to palate and made a short, excited yelp-cutt. He double-gobbled from the same spot, then gobbled again 30 seconds later much closer.

Gun up, barrel selector switched to the open-choked barrel, safety off. I had a wide shooting lane directly in front, but I knew the only part of it I'd be able to work with was the first few inches. He was going to be right on top of me when I saw him, and if I wasn't on him instantly it would be too late. He drummed right behind the cedar, maybe 10 yards away, and it gave me the edge I needed. I lowered my point of aim six inches at the sound, and half a second later he was there, out of strut and low-walking, looking, looking…

When a gobbler is that close and you are without a tree, whether you move or not doesn't really matter. You are going to be made. And I was, but that last-second barrel adjustment was spot on. He saw me and reversed direction, and my index finger slapped the trigger just as he disappeared behind the cedar. I knew it was a kill or a clean miss – there are no cripples at six yards – so I took my time as I picked up my cushion and stuffed it in my vest. No need for hurry; he was either laying there or he wasn't.

When I rounded the cedar, he was.

In addition to providing an exciting hunt, The Ankle Bracelet Gobbler carried a $100 reward tag. He'd been banded three months earlier and less than four miles away from where he died.

Chapter 14

The Gobblers of Hell Hollow

The secondary road runs more than six miles through a walk-in turkey hunting area. For three months, March through May, the gates on each end are locked. It's not so pretty in there anymore – a heavy-handed logging operation a few years ago took care of that – but when this Bad Bird encounter unfolded nearly 20 years ago, it was truly a gorgeous place.

My listening spot was two miles past the gate on the north end, a tater knob of a hill surrounded by downslopes in every direction. The two gobblers I heard from that knob on this particular morning, a week into the season, were farther south into the walk-in area, at the very limit of hearing, probably three-quarters of a mile away. They were across a deep, steep hollow and I really didn't want to go that far across the rough ground, but they were going at it pretty good. After 15 minutes passed and nobody gobbled closer, I gave in. I was younger then, and stupider.

It took me more than 30 minutes to cross that hellish hole and get into their neighborhood, and by then they were on the ground. It looked like a good situation, with relatively flat ground on my final approach and the turkeys far enough over the lip into the next hollow to let me get in tight. When I picked a tree and sat down, I was no more than 75 yards from the turkeys.

I didn't do anything at first. If they came far enough up the slope to let me see them, they'd be killable, and if they came up the slope on their own they wouldn't be looking for me. But it didn't work out, and when they started slowly drifting farther along the slope, I got into the game with some soft clucks and yelps. They were interested and it stopped their retreat, but they didn't come back my way. They were now 125 yards or so off the gun.

After a while I got up, retreated 50 yards from the edge of the flat and scooted past the two gobblers, who were making plenty enough noise for me to keep track of them. When I was as far ahead of them as I'd been behind, I eased as close to the edge of the slope as I dared and set up again. In the absence of any more calling from my last spot, the gobblers had resumed their slow drift along the face of the slope, slowly but surely heading my way. Again, I decided my best play was to stay silent.

Wait, did I just say *surely?* Correction. There are precious few "sure-lys" in turkey hunting, and this wasn't one of them. The turkeys closed to 80, maybe 90 yards, at which point I saw one pass through a little opening in the timber. Trouble was, he was no longer headed my way. Instead, he was going down the slope rather than side-hilling it, and seconds later I saw the second gobbler pass through the opening.

Time to play a card. I yelped smartly and loudly, then followed close behind it with a short but excited cutting series. Both gobblers walked all over it. I gave them another run of yelps and they cut my call again. Then I saw them, this time noticeably closer but still 25 yards too far. They stopped and scanned the open slope between us for several minutes, minutes that seemed like hours. Unless it's to make a gobbler stop walking or raise his head for the shot, I never call to a gobbler I'm looking at inside of a hundred yards. They can pinpoint the source of the sound too well, and the last thing I want is for a gobbler to be scrutinizing that suspicious-looking blob at the base of my tree.

So, as much as every cell in my body was screaming at me to do it, I kept my teeth firmly clamped together, locking the triple-reed cutter firmly against my palate. This stalemate, as mentioned, lasted several min-utes/hours, and when the turkeys didn't see what they were looking for they turned, did that soul-crushing wing shuffle, and walked down the slope again.

I gave them an extra two minutes (hours?) after they were gone and then hustled back to the top of the slope, moved another hundred yards along the rim and then dropped 200 yards straight downhill. They didn't seem to want to come up the slope. Maybe I could call them downhill.

But when I called from set number three, nobody bothered to answer. When they gobbled again after 20 minutes had crawled by, they were 300 yards away and near the bottom of the hollow.

I know when I'm beat. I also knew the hollow the turkeys had gone into was even worse than the one I'd just crossed. Armed with those two useful nuggets of knowledge, I gathered my stuff and climbed back up the steep slope. Then I crossed Hell Hollow and slowly worked my way back to the truck, calling as I went. I never heard a peep.

*   *   *

I hunted elsewhere the next three days. Heard a few turkeys but couldn't make anything happen. So against my better judgement, the next morning found me making that long pre-dawn hike to my tater knob listening spot. I didn't want to cross Hell Hollow again, but when the same two turkeys cranked up way over there and nothing gobbled any closer, I shook my head, shouldered my gun and dropped off into Hell.

Because I didn't wait as long before starting over there, I got to the turkeys while they were still in the tree. They were just down the slope of the next hollow, in a stand of pines at about eye level with the flat ground on top. I set up 100 yards south of them, in the direction they'd gone a few days ago, right on the break of the slope so I could have a chance at covering both approaches.

At first it looked like I'd outsmarted them. I didn't call any while they did their considerable amount of roost gobbling, and when they flew down they did it in my direction. I heard them leave the limb and caught a glimpse of one of them sailing toward me. He landed just out of sight behind a boulder outcropping on the flat, 60 yards away. I was sucking in air to give him a cluck or two when the second gobbler sailed in behind him. He landed close to his buddy, but far enough to the right to be within my sight. Rats. I reminded myself: *Never call to a visible turkey that's not killable yet.*

So I didn't.

The visible turkey looked around, and when his buddy behind the rock let loose a ferocious gobble he answered with an equally ferocious one. He walked behind the boulders and I heard the purring sequence that usually accompanies a gobbler fight. But there was no wing-flapping and the purring only lasted a few seconds. When it stopped, I got my gun up and made a short cut/yelp call.

Your guess is as good as mine where those gobblers went, but I stayed over there until noon and that was the last I heard or saw of them that day. I waited a solid hour with my gun on my knee, and when I stood up and slowly stalked to the boulder pile, the ground beyond it was as innocent of turkeys as a city park tennis court.

*   *   *

I laid off of them for two days this time, but after again failing to find a turkey that wanted to die I was back at the tater knob at first light. At the first gobble from across Hell Hollow I was off the knob and headed that way.

They weren't far from where they'd been the second day I hunted them, but the roosting situation was different. They were on top of the flat this time, in timber too sparse for me to get very close. I set up 150 yards south, and given the conditions, that was pushing the envelope.

Maybe pushing it a little too far. The turkeys kept gobbling after I sat to them, but they flew down north instead of south like they'd been doing, and after gobbling a little on the ground they kept moving that direction. I fell in behind, and you don't need me to tell you how that played out. When they quit gobbling and I lost them, it was 10:30 and they'd taken me a mile further from the truck.

These two gobblers were fast getting on my nerves, but they were also getting under my skin. You know how it is. You're morally certain you're not going to kill anything, but you're the moth and the gobbler is the flame and, to adjust a line from my old friend Tom Kelly, you are helpless in the grip of your compulsion.

*   *   *

I had one more day to hunt in Arkansas before leaving for an out-of-state swing. In for a penny, in for a pound, and that final morning found me leaving the house an hour earlier than normal. A full half-hour before dawn made its first crack I was across Hell Hollow, sitting on a flat-topped rock on the flat, waiting for the gobblers to crank up.

About 15 yards behind my sitting rock were two big pines. Guess where the gobblers were roosted? The first clue was when one of them greeted the graying eastern sky with a rip-roaring gobble into my left ear. Seconds later his buddy assaulted my right ear.

I was pinned down like a coon hide on a barn wall. There I sat, on a rock 20 feet from the nearest tree, which was where I'd leaned my gun before sitting on the rock. I had two turkeys in trees 15 yards behind me. My vest, with my gloves, head neat and all my calls, was over there beside my gun. A more unfavorable scenario I cannot imagine, unless maybe there could have been a rattlesnake between my feet.

I couldn't do anything but sit there and hope they wouldn't notice me. Normally, I thrill at the sound of a turkey's gobble, especially at close range. But this particular situation put all that to the test. The turkeys were really in fine form, and they decided to hold a gobbling contest. I have no idea how many times they gobbled, but I do know how long they did it: 90 minutes from the first gobble until they finally – *finally* – pitched out over my head. They sailed close enough I felt the wind, and lit side by side within gun range. But you already know where my gun was, and it wasn't loaded anyway.

As was mentioned earlier in this tale of woe, I know when I'm beat. Since there was no tomorrow to hunt these two turkeys, I did a thing I'd never done before and have never done since. I waited until the two turkeys made their first on-the-ground gobbles of the morning, sounding off in quick succession as was their custom…and then I leapt to my feet and shouted, "Get the hell out of here!" at the top of my lungs.

They did. So did I.

Chapter 15

The Lineman (Again)

It's been sold and subdivided into five-acre ranchettes now, but one of Jill's favorite turkey spots used to be a 300-acre tract of steep, heavily-timbered Ozark foothill country bisected by two high-voltage power line rights-of-way. The third or fourth year she hunted the place, she met and was soundly beaten by a gobbler that earned both a name and a chapter in *Bad Birds 2*. You can read that entire story in Chapter 23 of that book, but here's the Cliff Notes version:

For various reasons, The Lineman whipped her four days in a row, while I was suffering through my own drubbing from another Bad Bird several miles away. I needed a break from my turkey but Jill was mad at hers, so for the next two days we double-teamed him with no success. That second day of our double-team effort, Jill actually sat down under the gobbler's roost tree. We hunted him two or three more days that season as a team, and Jill went to him a few more times after I'd washed my hands of him, but when we left the state for our customary May state-hopping road trip, he was still holding court along those parallel rights-of-way.

*　　*　　*

Late the next March when we started seriously scouting our

local birds, The Lineman was still there. He'd picked up a subordinate buddy since last year, and he still seemed to prefer roosting in one of two small hollows that headed up between the power lines and a state highway that paralleled them. We checked him six or seven days during our three-week scouting period, and every time he and his buddy were roosted in the head of one or the other of those hollows, so close to the roadway I don't see how in the world they got any sleep.

If it hadn't been for that highway, he might have been an easy turkey. (Emphasis on "might".) The problem was, there was less than 75 yards between the asphalt and the first power line cut, so there wasn't enough room to set up above this bird when he was still on the roost. Besides, who wants to set up on a turkey so close to a busy highway you can feel the vibrations of the passing 18-wheelers? Not much of a quality outdoor experience, to my way of thinking.

But Jill still had a good mad-on for this particular turkey, and there was only one possibility for her on Opening Day. But I'd already washed my hands of him the season before, and I was determined I wasn't going to dirty them again. So I made my own hunt while Jill went to the power lines, and her first hunt of the new season went more or less as follows:

The Lineman was in the left-hand hollow that morning. For some reason the other turkey wasn't with him; he'd roosted a quarter-mile away down the power lines and was gobbling about a third as much. Jill went up the right-hand hollow and got even with The Lineman, then slipped to the crown of the ridge separating the two holes. At this point she was about 125 yards from the gobbler. She couldn't pick him out in the tree, but she was pretty sure she had the tree pinpointed. Sure enough, she saw him fly down from that tree, and the hopeful thing was, he flew in her direction, landing in or near the bottom of the hollow. This would have put him less than 75 yards away.

The Lineman was a proven Bad Bird, but it wasn't because he didn't like to gobble. He stayed down there in the hollow and carried on a conversation with my wife for more than an hour before a real hen showed up and stole him away. He continued to gobble for the next three hours, not as much as before but enough to keep Jill from giving up on him. She tagged along behind that turkey for most of the morning. The subordinate bird had shut up. "If I'd heard another turkey gobbling, I'd have gone to him in a heartbeat," she told me later that day. "But I didn't have any other options."

Falling in behind a gobbler that already has at least one hen is a sucker bet, and both Jill and I know it. The thing is, though, it works just often enough to keep people like us trying it. And like Jill said, it was the only game in town. Having a gobbler answer your calling beats quitting early, every single time. Even if the gobbler in question is gobbling at you over his shoulder.

Which this one was, and it led her around all morning before shutting up himself, leaving my wife standing in the suddenly quiet woods with frustration on her face and ugly words in her mouth.

*   *   *

I realize this is a story about Jill and The Lineman, but I simply don't have the discipline to not tell you about my own hunt that morning:

My game plan was to check out three small private properties we sometimes hunted. I gave each a good workout, heard a couple birds on the second place but wasn't able to get on them properly, and by 11:30 I'd struck out on all three tracts. Then the wind came up, really howling, and I decided to call it a day.

I was less than 10 minutes from the house when I drove by a small public area where a truck had been parked at daylight. The truck was gone, and on a whim I pulled in.

I'd stopped along the way for a Coke and a package of peanut butter crackers. The crackers were gone but I still had a crumb-y

121

mouth, so I grabbed my box call and stepped out of the truck. The parking area was on an exposed hillside and the wind made me think of turkey hunting in western Oklahoma. I set my Coke on the hood of the still-idling vehicle and racked off the loudest set of yelps and cuts that box call is capable of making. When the turkey gobbled he wasn't 40 yards away, behind a screen of brush in the edge of the woods next to the parking spot. If the wind hadn't been blowing at near gale force, he'd have spooked at my truck's engine.

I was thunderstruck. I left the driver door open, left the truck running, grabbed my shotgun out of the back seat and dashed 25 yards behind the truck and ducked into the woods. I ran another 20 feet and fell down beside a gnarly blackjack oak not as big around as a cantaloupe. Here is a list of the things I had with me:

  --one over-under shotgun

  --two shotgun shells

  --one box call

That's it. No seat cushion, no vest, no hat, no gloves. I didn't even have a face mask.

So there I was, shotgun in one hand and box call in the other. I was already panicked, and I doubled down on it: I threw the box call down like it was a rattlesnake. The call went *squawk!* when it landed, and the gobbler roared at it. I snatched the gun to my face just as the bird rounded the screen of brush and I shot him at 17 yards.

From opening the truck door to pulling the trigger couldn't possibly have taken more than 45 seconds, and I'm guessing it was closer to 30. I still tell that story as often as I can, to whomever I can get to hold still for it.

*   *   *

All right, please excuse that detour, and thanks for letting me tell it one more time. I made the mistake of telling it to Jill about 15 minutes after it happened – we arrived home at almost the same time. I was still riding the adrenaline high, and I quickly discovered she wasn't in the mood for it. She and I always congratulate each other when we fill a tag, and to her credit, she kept the tradition alive that day. But to say her heart wasn't in it would be serious understatement.

"Well, he's a very nice turkey and that's a very nice story." That's how I remember what she said, but the smile on her lips didn't reach her eyes. That was the last thing she said for a while.

Later that day, though, after she quit being quite so sore at me, she said she wanted me to hunt The Lineman with her the next day. Here's the way I remember that conversation: "At this point, I don't care whether I kill him, or you kill him, or he tries to cross the highway and gets run over by a school bus. I just want him to die, and two hunters have a better chance of killing him than one."

I really wanted to go back for a try at the two turkeys I'd heard, but you know what they say about choosing your battles. Since it wasn't a hill I wanted to die on, I gave the proper husbandly answer: "Yes, dear. I'd be pleased to hunt The Lineman with you tomorrow."

* * *

We roosted The Lineman that night. He and his buddy went up on the small ridge between his two favored roosting hollows, and the second dawn of the new turkey season found us sitting 125 yards apart, where the south power line crossed the two hollows. I was on the high ground west of the west hollow, looking east. Jill was on the high ground east of the east hollow, looking west. Unless he crossed the highway or stayed on the middle ridge – neither of which was in his usual M.O. – we figured one of us had a good chance at him.

We'd agreed to stay quiet for a while to see what would happen. The Lineman hadn't acted like a call-shy turkey, exactly – he usually gobbled when you called to him – but he seemed exceptionally cagey.

And since we had a pretty good double-team set-up on him, we decided to hunt him like he was a deer.

Like clockwork, he started gobbling right after we heard the first cardinal. His buddy again chimed in, but didn't say much. It was tough (for me, at least) to keep from tree calling to him, but I managed. It was tougher to resist calling after he got on the ground, but again I managed. He and his buddy lit on the middle ridge. I saw them in the air but couldn't see them on the ground, but no matter. He was in rare form that day, and he gobbled close to a hundred times on the limb and another 50 in the first 15 minutes after flydown. From the sound of it, he was staying right where his feet touched the ground. Two hollows over, Jill was managing to lay off her calling, too. She told me later she'd seen both of them in the air, too, but had also lost sight when they touched down.

After those 50 gobbles, she sent me a text: *What do we do?*

I sent back: *Do I look like Brad Harris?*

No. He's skinnier than you.

That hurt. It was the truth, but it still hurt.

Another 15 minutes. Another 50 gobbles from the same spot. Another text from Jill:

Seriously. What do we do?

I don't know. Stick to the plan I guess. We move closer we bump him, we back off we leave the front door open.

I don't like it.

So sue me. You come up with a plan, then.

Pbbbttthttt!

The Lineman gobbled in place for another 20 minutes and then abruptly shut up. He didn't taper off, he just quit cold turkey. Yes, that was a pun.

I don't know how he got past us without getting seen. The right of way wasn't like a lawn by any means, but the grass was short and the bushes were scattered and small. Both of us could see the whole of it

Mike Handley

The Lineman picked up a running buddy the second year Jill hunted him, but we couldn't kill him, either.

between our relative positions, and yet when he started gobbling again he was past both power lines and into the brushy woods beyond.

My phone buzzed. *How did he do that?*

I didn't answer, just stood up, stretched my numb legs and walked out into the open. Jill saw me and joined me out there.

"You want to go after him?" she asked.

"Be my guest. Take your time. I'm going to go see about those turkeys I heard on Pete's place yesterday. Call me if you kill him and I'll come pick you up."

She chased him. She stayed in contact with him until noon. She didn't kill him. I didn't kill either of the gobblers I'd heard at Pete's, either. Considering Jill's reaction to my 30-second bird the day before, that was probably a good thing.

Typical turkey hunting. If it was easy, women and children would be out there doing it. And before you women and youth hunters jump down my throat for saying that, you need to know it was my wife, Jill Easton, email jllljeaston@gmail.com, who said it first.

* * *

We were in Arkansas for another six days. Jill hunted The Lineman five of them. I didn't. Neither of us killed another turkey, and when we left for Missouri we drove past his roosting hollows on the state highway.

"I'll never hunt that turkey again," Jill said.

And she never did. I think she would have reneged on her promise, but in June a developer went in there with bulldozers, chain saws and survey flags. By spring there were four houses under construction in The Lineman's playground. One of them was directly in The Lineman's customary landing zone – on the middle ridge between the two roosting hollows, 75 yards from the state highway.

Don't tell Jill this, but I was relieved.

Chapter 16

The Drug Runner Gobblers

It was your typical south Texas hunting operation: hot, powderhouse dry, gray-brown mesquite brush everywhere. The ranch, near Encino, Texas, had 1100 acres of high fence and sold hunts for the usual mix of African imports – oryx, zebra, blackbuck, maybe some other stuff – as well as Pere David's deer from China, a relatively unusual south Texas exotic. There were also the native whitetails and javelina. And hogs, naturally. There's not an acre of rural south Texas without hog tracks on it.

And of course, turkeys. Jill and I had booked an early spring hunt with this outfitter on the recommendation of our friend Dale. But between Dale's hunt and ours, the long-time owner/outfitter had died and the hunts were now being run by his son Kyle, an incompetent twenty-something with a cell phone permanently attached to his left hand and the personality and people skills of a bois d'arc fence post. I won't burden you with the gory details, but let's say young Kyle had a lot to learn about being an outfitter.

The place had turkeys, I'll say that. Good thing, too, because here's the intel Kyle gave us when he dropped us off in the pre-dawn blackness the first morning. This is an exact quote: "Turkeys have been roosting back that way. (*Ambiguous wave of the arm that covered about 90 degrees of the compass.*) You ought to hear something from here. Call me when you want me to pick you up." And then he drove away, back to camp – it was a very nice camp, by the way – presumably to commune with his cell phone.

Now, understand me here. I am a dedicated public land turkey hunter, and neither Jill nor I are the kind of hunters who need somebody to hold our hand on a turkey hunt. Both of us are perfectly capable of finding turkeys and screwing up our chances on them without any outside help. But when you are paying $3000 for a two-person hunt, part of what you're paying for is intellience. It was an unguided hunt; we didn't expect anybody to seat us in a blind and parade a string of longbeards past us until we found a couple we liked. But something beyond "You ought to hear something from here" would have been nice.

For what it was worth, though, Kyle was right. We heard turkeys gobbling "back that way." But we didn't know the lay of the land back that way – he hadn't bothered to inform us – so the best we could do was follow a sandy, two-track sendero that led in the general direction of the gobbling.

The turkeys were on the ground by the time we figured out how to get close, and as we closed the distance we came to a big field/food plot that would have been green as Irish underwear anywhere except south Texas. Here, it was dry, brownish-yellow sand, with wispy sprigs of what appeared to be stunted wheat emerging here and there. In a few places the wheat was thick enough to give the ground a wash of anemic green, but mostly it was just a sprig or two here and there or bare, dusty ground.

Still, it was the best-looking turkey location we'd seen, so we found a spot in the brush at the edge of the opening and called to the turkeys that were still gobbling in the middle distance. They were maybe 500 yards away, and we could have easily gotten a lot closer with all the thick mesquite to hide our approach. But we didn't know if there was any place open enough to provide a decent set-up.

Things looked promising at first. The distant turkeys immediately answered our yelps, and within minutes we could tell at least some of them were headed our way. We traded turkey conversation with them for a while and eventually we could tell there were at least three gobblers in the group, maybe four. Whatever their strength, they were making lots of noise, and they were now less than a hundred yards away.

Between us, however, was the thickest mesquite tangle I've seen. It didn't look like a rabbit could get through it, much less a turkey gobbler. Visibility in that direction was measured in feet, not yards… and not very many feet, either. Jill and I formulated a plan. We'd sit back-to-back where we were, a few feet into the brush, and cover both approaches along the edge. We figured it was safe to assume they wouldn't come through that thick brush.

Our assumption might have been safe, but it was also wrong. The turkeys hadn't gobbled for several minutes, and we sat alert with our guns shouldered, steadying each other by the pressure of our backs. Two turkey hunters functioning as one, cocked and ready for whatever the next few minutes might bring.

Except we weren't ready for the turkeys to come at us through the thick brush, and that's exactly what they did. I was covering the right-hand approach, so I had my left shoulder to the field when I heard a questioning *cluck?* from just off my right shoulder. I turned my head slowly and was looking at the right spot purely by accident when a gobbler's head appeared in it, less than ten feet away. Then a second head lined up behind the first, and then a third. While I was looking at them, they gobbled in unison, three turkey heads darting out in three directions, like some kind of synchronized songfest.

It was fascinating at that close range, but it was also startling and I guess I flinched. The brush blew up, and three adult gobblers boiled out of it like a small covey of gigantic quail. Just as much as them coming through it in the first place, I was surprised they were able to fly up out of it. As with most things turkeys do when they're alarmed, it didn't take them long to make their getaway.

We sat there a few minutes, regrouping, waiting for our heart rates to get back to normal. Some of the gobblers we'd heard on the roost were still making themselves heard "back that way," and a sendero exited the field in that direction. We followed it, and it led to a smaller, L-shaped field. The turkeys were gobbling around the corner of the L. It broke to the right, and we approached along the inside edge of our part of the field until the corner was well within shotgun range. We again set up in the brush at the edge of the open ground and started calling.

We got a pretty good back-and-forth going with the two gobblers around the corner, and they seemed to be approaching the corner where we'd be able to see them. Their gobbles were still 50 yards from that point, however, when a mob of either 16 or 17 gangly jakes came running past us from behind, across the field and out of sight into the mesquite. The gobbling stopped. A minute later we heard human voices, indistinct but unmistakable as human, back where the jakes had come from. It sounded like Spanish.

The voices were audible for maybe five minutes, moving south to north through the heavy brush a hundred yards or so west of the field. Odd. Why fight your way through heavy cover when…

That's when the *aha!* moment came. Item 1: We were in south Texas, not terribly close to the border but not that far, either. Item 2: Spanish-speaking people by the multiplied thousands were walking cross-country, heading north. Item 3: Aforementioned Spanish-speaking people were avoiding openings like fields and senderos. One plus two plus three equaled illegal immigrants at best, drug traffickers at worst. We weren't eager to encounter either, so we sat quietly for the next 30 minutes, listening and watching. We didn't hear anything else, from people nor turkeys.

By now it was 10:00. I had an appointment at 10:45 to do a

radio interview to promote *Bad Birds 2*, so I left Jill at the edge of the small field and walked back toward the larger field so I could talk without disturbing her hunt. There in the dust of the sendero were three sets of tracks crossing the road, overlaid on the tracks Jill and I had laid down only an hour before.

I was looking at them when three o.d. green-uniformed men carrying sidearms and AR-15s came around a bend in the trail. We saw each other at the same time and I raised my arms away from my sides, my shotgun hanging from my shoulder by its sling.

"I'm a turkey hunter," I said. The three men, who had stiffened and stopped when they saw me, relaxed a little. "You guys Border Patrol?"

The team leader answered in the affirmative. "Do you mind unloading your gun?"

I complied. "You looking for somebody?"

Affirmative again. I motioned them forward, showed them the tracks crossing ours. "These are the tracks my wife and I made about 9 o'clock. These guys came across the road sometime after that."

I told them about hearing the Spanish-speaking voices and approximately where we'd heard them. They asked about Jill's location and I told them, told them why I'd come back this way, told them everything I could think of.

"We're on our way to link up with four other agents in this enclosure," the leader said. "We've been after these three men since daylight, and the other team is in position to intercept them on the north end of the property. When you get through with your phone call, please return to where you left your wife. You can keep hunting, but please don't go any farther north on the property today. Thanks for your help." And within seconds they were gone, following the tracks of the three illegals into the mesquite.

The radio interview I did shortly afterwards was the most illogical, rambling interview I've ever done. After it ended, I eased back to where I'd left Jill, and when I got close she motioned for me to hurry.

"Get in here and be quiet," she whispered. "Two turkeys just gobbled right around the corner of the field, not two minutes before you got here."

We waited. Nothing happened.

"Have you called to 'em?" I asked, after five minutes crawled by.

"No. I was about to when you showed up." I gave her the T.K. and Mike finger roll.

She carved three soft yelps off the sounding board of her Lynch box call, and the last note was still in the air when the two gobblers answered from no more than 50 feet away. You guessed it: they were in the thick brush behind us. Looked like it was going to be another in-your-face encounter, but at least we had two guns this time and advance warning of where they were.

Fat lot of good it did us. The turkeys gobbled again a few minutes later, and they were still in the thick stuff but 50 yards past us. They stepped into the field 75 yards away, gobbled again and walked away down the sendero at the end of the food plot, despite our team effort calling.

"You think we ought to go after them?" Jill asked. I told her about my encounter with the Border Patrol folks. We decided our best play was to sit tight and not run the risk of interfering with the pursuit of the illegals. So we sat for the next three hours, and turkeys came by us twice – a lone hen, and about 30 minutes behind her, the big mob of jakes that had run past us earlier. This time they weren't running, so we got an accurate count: Eighteen.

At two o'clock we called Kyle. Enough excitement for one day. (We found out later the Border Patrol guys had corralled the three illegals. They were carrying a substantial amount of fentanyl.)

*   *   *

Our "host" wanted to put us out at the same place the second morning, but we vetoed that. We told him to drop us on the road halfway between the two fields we'd visited the first morning. For some reason Kyle didn't like that idea, but by then neither Jill nor I gave a damn what Kyle didn't like. We were stuck with him for the remainder of this hunt, but we didn't have to do things on his terms.

Kyle dropped us without saying a word and drove off stony-faced down the dusty sendero. And thus, our second day at the Encino property started on another sour note.

It didn't get any better. I have mentioned the ranch has zebras. I neglected, though, to mention how many. The answer is, a *bunch*. For some reason they didn't bother us at all the first day, but on Day Two they sure made up for it.

What zebras will do, we learned that morning, is bark at you when they smell you. It doesn't really sound like a dog's bark, but I don't know how else to describe it. And a zebra's bark is every bit as detrimental to a turkey hunt as the blowing of a whitetail deer. (Which, by the way, also chimed in a few times that second morning.)

We covered a lot of ground that day and set up on four groups of gobbling turkeys and one gobbler we think was by himself. Zebras messed us up on two of the groups, whitetails did it on a third. I have no idea what went wrong on the other two. All I know for sure is no turkeys came in. After the fifth encounter fizzled at 2 p.m., we gave it up for the day and called our BFF Kyle.

*   *   *

While we were traveling around the property that second day, we found numerous places where illegals had discarded things on their way north – water bottles and jugs, mostly, but also empty food containers (beans, Vienna sausage, candy wrappers) and stuff like worn-out t-shirts, dirty diapers, blown-out flip-flops and used toilet paper. It was obvious the place was a regularly-used travel corridor for Biden's favorite people – a fact Kyle hadn't bothered to mention when we booked the hunt or when we arrived.

So the third morning, blessedly our last day at this ranch, we decided to go to the L-shaped field and just stay there until we either killed something or until we got all of it we wanted. Moving and hunting hadn't paid off, and we figured our chance of encountering illegals was lowest if we sat on a field and didn't roam around.

Turkeys started gobbling at the customary time, and although we could hear five or six of them scattered around, none were close and we stuck to our game plan. At about eight o'clock a gobbler followed a lone hen across the field, but he was 75 yards away and wasn't interested in leaving a hen he could see for a hen that he couldn't. We understood his reasoning, but that didn't make it any less frustrating. Two hours later we were debating about calling Kyle and cutting our losses on this hunt. We had another Texas hunt booked 200 miles away starting the next day, and to say we were ready to put Encino and Kyle in the rear-view mirror would have been a serious understatement. We decided to give it another hour and quit at eleven a.m.

At 10:47, there was a cluster-gobble down the sendero behind us, sounding like a half-dozen or more turkeys. We figured it was a bunch of jakes but turned around and got ready anyway, and we barely got settled in again when a group of eight longbeards came boiling into the field like a high school sophomore baseball team coming out of the dugout. They were 50 yards away when we saw them and five seconds later they were at 35 and closing fast.

"Better shoot before they get too close," I whispered. She shot immediately and a turkey went down. When we have a chance to double on turkeys, our invariable rule is that Jill shoots first (forget about that one-two-three-shoot thing) and then I come in for clean-up if the opportunity presents. This time, nothing presented. The seven surviving turkeys, rather than flogging their downed companion the way they often do, broke and ran back down the sendero, and I couldn't get a clear shot because of brush and my wife's head being in the way. She hates it when I shoot her head off.

I called Kyle, told him to pick us up. When Jill put her big two-year-old gobbler in the back of his truck, he never said a word.

Author's note: Our next Texas hunt, with Johnathan Freeman of TurkeyHuntCo, was exceptional. What a difference a personable outfitter makes!

Chapter 17

The Crazy Gobbler
of Crazy Bayou

"Inside the levee."

Say those words around any turkey hunter in Arkansas, Louisiana or Mississippi and you're immediately going to have their undivided attention. That's what turkey hunters in those states collectively call the lands between the lower Mississippi River and the huge, extensive series of earthen levees that flank the river and hold it in during times of flood.

"Inside the levee" is Holy Grail country. It's the Mecca toward which southern turkey hunters genuflect. Almost 100% timbered, much of it is still owned by big lumber companies or land holding companies. Almost every acre is tied up in private, high-dollar hunting leases, and if you need to ask how much a membership costs, never mind. You can't afford it.

But if you have the right good friend, you don't need a membership. My old friend Sid, God rest his soul, was the right good friend. He was already a member of one of those big leases when Truman became president. He inherited his membership from his father, one of the founding members. Sid's membership number, like his father's before him, was 1.

Sid was one of the few members who had a cabin on the lease, and for most of the year he lived there. And every year, for a week or so in early April, so did I.

The Camp – that's all Sid ever called it, The Camp – sat on the bank of a little landlocked slough known by the membership as Crazy Bayou. Nobody ever told me why. Home mostly to greenback turtles, perch, grinnel and gar, it effectively cut off access to the large expanse of woods on the other side. You could boat across the bayou from Sid's yard, but the opposite bank was steep, and getting to the top was tricky. You could drive around and get there on a series of barely improved roads, but even then you had to park almost a mile from Sid's cabin, and there were several smaller sloughs to cross before you got to the slough bank behind The Camp. Sometimes they were dry. Usually they weren't.

Looking across Crazy Bayou from The Camp, it was a beautiful stretch of woods. Once you got over there, though, the understory was thick and so was the midstory, which is unusual for lower Mississippi River inside the levee woods. It wasn't impassable; you could get around in there if you took your time and didn't try to walk a compass course. But all that low-growing stuff made it hard to see an approaching turkey. Or an approaching bull elephant, for that matter.

So when I went to The Camp, I hunted other places. With 19,000 acres and only a handful of serious turkey hunters in the lease, there were lots of other places.

Except for that one year…

See, inside the levee turkeys have a boom or bust lifestyle, depending on whether the Mississippi floods in April and May. If it doesn't, there's almost always a good hatch. If you get a few consecutive years of high water during nesting time, though, the hatch is poor. Floods don't leave much dry ground for nesting, and what little there is, is crowded with egg-eating predators trying to escape the water. This year I'm talking about was following three straight springs of high water, and Sid's lease was running few to the hill on adult gobblers.

But the water was down, or at least lower, when turkey season opened that fourth year, and if you were lucky enough to find a gobbler, you could hunt it without worrying too much about water hazards. Trouble was, the only gobbling turkey I could locate that wasn't being hunted by others was, you guessed it: across that water hazard known as Crazy Bayou, right behind The Camp.

*   *   *

So the second morning I shoved Sid's creaky, leaky old 12-foot johnboat down the slick bank and sculled across the scummy surface of Crazy Bayou. It was no walk in the park getting up that steep bank, made even more difficult because it had rained during the night. By the time I made the top I was muddy as a stinkpot turtle, and Sid was standing in his back yard laughing like a maniac. Quietly, to be sure, because Sid was a turkey hunter too, but laughing like a maniac nonetheless.

I gave him the universal hand sign of displeasure and walked into the woods. Thirty seconds later I heard his truck start as he left for his own hunt. My turkey gobbled at the rumbling diesel, and good thing he did because I'd have walked under him in the next 100 yards. It was still pretty dusky so I was okay for the moment, but moving any closer to the gobbler was foolhardy and the groundline vegetation was too heavy to set up where I was.

I backed up 30 yards, then worked my way through the brush to my left, moving east toward the river. I wanted the sun at my back and in the gobbler's eyes if I could find a spot where I had a decent sight distance. The best I could find, though, was a spot along a small slough that had three or four inches of water in it. If I set up with my back to the slough, I had 25 to 30 yards of visibility in the half-circle in front of me. In these thick woods, I figured it was the best I was going

139

to do. The gobbler was more than 150 yards from me. I wanted to be closer, but the water in the slough would provide a good backstop and maybe prevent the gobbler from circling to get the sun out of his eyes.

Anyway, the slow circle I'd made halfway around the gobbler had used up more time than I wanted it to, and I told myself it was about time for him to fly down. Which is precisely what he did, just as I put my seat cushion on the ground and was preparing to sit. I didn't hear him leave the limb, but his next gobble was more muffled than his earlier ones and came from a different direction. He was on the ground, and I still hadn't announced my presence.

Still standing, I gave him an excited but short burst, a call I make often that consists of a couple of quick yelps breaking over into a cutting sequence and finishing off with a couple more yelps. He broke into the back half of it with a double gobble. Not a bad way to start a hunt, and I felt smug as I settled onto my cushion, raked some leaves away, made sure the gun was loaded, laid out a couple friction calls and did all that stuff you do when the battle is imminent but has not yet been joined.

Spoiler alert: I wouldn't have felt nearly as smug if I'd known that double gobble was the high point of the hunt. I let him simmer for a minute or two while I was getting ready to take him on, during which time he gobbled six or seven more times. He didn't seem to be in a hurry to go anywhere, but I knew that could change in a heartbeat. I got my gun comfortably propped on my knee and did a gentle, *where-are-you?* yelp. He answered me immediately, and when he gobbled again 30 seconds later, he was noticeably closer.

I wanted to call again – man oh man, did I want to call again! – but he was already coming, and he was looking for me. I didn't want to give him the same case of overconfidence I was currently dealing with, so I somehow managed to remain silent. He gobbled again after another minute or three, and he was closer yet but farther to my right, almost to the bank of the slough I was sitting on. I shifted around while I still had time.

That was the last I heard of him until that suspicious *cluck!* came from straight out in front, which is where I'd had my gun pointed until I shifted position five minutes ago. Now, though, he was 90 degrees off my barrel. Often I lack the self-control for situations like this, but for once I kept myself from flinching when he clucked in my left ear. I cut my eyes as far that way as I could without moving my head but couldn't find him. It took me a full minute to slowly turn my head that direction, and still I couldn't pick him out. I held that position for 15 minutes. The only thing I got out of it was a crick in my neck.

When he finally gobbled again. letting me relax and turn my head to a more comfortable position, he was 250 yards past me along the slough. He gobbled once more 20 minutes later, and I could barely hear him. I got closer and we conversed a little, but nothing came of it. He quit gobbling at 11, and since nothing else was within hearing range, I headed back to Crazy Bayou.

After one of Sid's pint fruit-jar Bloody Marys and his locally famous BELT sandwiches (a standard BLT with a hard-fried egg added; lay a slice of cheese on the egg and it becomes a BELTCH; add a slab of sweet onion and you've got a BELTCHO,) a nap was indicated.

No, not indicated. The correct word here is "necessary." I ate not one but two BELTCHOs, and Sid refilled my fruit jar halfway through the second one. As I recall, it was a splendid nap.

Late that afternoon, after a supper of fried pork chops, mashed potatoes, gravy, biscuits and corn on the cob – you didn't go to The Camp and not eat to the point of gluttony – I again crossed Crazy Bayou and sat down to listen.

He gobbled about 20 minutes before sundown, way back in there and far south of me. There wasn't enough time left to get on him and make a hunt, but I needed to figure out where he was. I took off in that direction. I'll spare you the details, but he never gobbled again, I didn't figure out where he was, and dark caught me a long way from The Camp and in a place I'd never been. I had a flashlight, but the brush I'd been going through pulled my compass on its shoestring lanyard out of my vest. All that was left was the string, with a pigtail at the end to show where the knot had come untied.

My bones would probably still be back in that brush if Sid hadn't started honking his truck's horn about 30 minutes after full dark. Even with that sound guiding me, it still took me almost an hour to get back. And for the rest of his life, Sid told that story every time he got me cornered around any of his numerous buddies.

*   *   *

The next morning, having no clue where the turkey was other than "way back in there," I elected to drive around and come in from the woods road south of the brushy tract that held the gobbler. I was pretty sure he was closer to the road than to Crazy Bayou.

Sure enough, he was, but when I parked my truck on the muddy access road and struck out through the woods in his direction, I soon hit another one of those sloughs. This one had more than a few inches of water in it. Way more. I tried wading but stopped when the water reached my waist. It was getting deeper with each step, and I was less than a third of the way across. Until then in my turkey hunting career, I had never swum to a turkey. Now, 35 years after that day, I can still make that claim.

I tried to get around the slough, but this was in the pre- hunting app days and I didn't know how long the slough was or which end of it was closest. In my ignorance I guessed wrong and went west. It led me away from the turkey, which by now was gobbling pretty good. I reversed direction and learned the slough ended less than 300 yards east of where I'd tried to cross it. By the time I learned that, however, the gobbler had made landfall and was on the move, heading cross-country back in the general direction of The Camp. He was gobbling every 30 to 45 seconds. I angled through the woods trying to intercept him and wonder of wonders, I succeeded. I found myself directly in his line of travel, maybe 150 yards ahead of him.

It was very brushy and I wouldn't have picked it as a set-up spot in a thousand years, but the turkey was moving through the stuff and it didn't seem to be deterring him. So I made my stand, but instead of sitting (which I tried, and found almost zero visibility,) I leaned my upper body into the pebbly bark of a big hackberry and stood to the turkey. It wasn't a great deal better, but I had a visibility range of from 20 to 25 yards in all directions. In turkey hunting, you play the hand you're dealt.

I was ahead of him, but I have mentioned before that this was brushy woods, and thick undergrowth tends to make any traveling critter larger than a fox squirrel weave and bob while traveling through it. When it seemed the turkey was going to miss me, against my better judgement I yelped at him with my mouth call when he was still about 125 yards out. I timed it so the sound of my call would reach his ears at the end of his gobble, and it stopped his drift. But it also stopped his feet. The next dozen gobbles he made all came from the same place, not quite a hundred yards west of me. The brushy terrain between us seemed slightly more open than the surroundings, and that again gave me that smug feeling. He'd eventually break, I was sure of it.

He did, but not the way I expected. I yelped at him again, he gobbled at it, and then he walked in a complete circle around me, about 40 to 50 yards out the whole time. He gobbled every 20 seconds and was killable the entire time. I kept circling the tree to keep it between us as much as possible, but I never caught a glimpse of him. He circled me not once but twice, gobbling and drumming nonstop, and then continued along his original track toward The Camp. I tried to flank him and get ahead of him again, but he was moving too fast for me to gain that much ground on him. I lost him about 11 o'clock. When I did

I was in a place I recognized – the bank of the same little slough where I'd set up on him the previous morning. I even found my set-up tree.

"I never heard of a turkey doing that," Sid said as I munched on my BELTCHO two hours later. "That bird is crazy." And presto, there was his name.

That afternoon a pop-up thunderstorm wandered over us and camped out, and between 3 p.m. and dark it rained more than two inches. I like turkey hunting about as much as anybody on the planet, but I do not go out in thunderstorms to hunt them. We spent the afternoon driving around in the rain on the roads that had enough sand and gravel to allow us passage. We saw enough deer to feed a batallion, but no turkeys.

*   *   *

The next morning I crossed Crazy Bayou and climbed that damnably slick bank, but this time I had the aid of the knotted rope I'd tied to a tree on top the day before. It still wasn't easy, but it didn't give Sid any cause for merriment. I walked quickly to the slough and stopped to listen beside my set-up tree.

The Crazy Gobbler of Crazy Bayou did not disappoint. He opened up while it was still dark, with no provocation at all. He was across the shallow slough, 250 yards behind me. It sounded like he was close to a football field sized tupelo brake I knew was only a quarter-mile from the road that ran along the river bank, and I waded the now foot-deep slough and squished my way closer.

Sure enough, he was roosted in the tupelo gum trees over the black water of the brake. I waited until I had enough light to move through the woods quietly, then circled halfway around the brake to get to the side of it where he was roosted. I figured that would give me the best odds of being close to where he'd fly down.

But Sid had named this gobbler accurately. He didn't fly out on the side he was closest to. Oh noooooo, his name was Crazy; he couldn't do anything that logical. Instead, he flew the entire length of the brake, dodging the dense tupelo trunks like a woodcock, and sailed far out over the brushy understory before disappearing from sight. When he gobbled on the ground I could barely hear him, and before I could even begin to gain on him he shut up.

Rather than trying to catch up to a silent gobbler from behind, I elected to take serious rounders on him. I hustled back to The Camp, drove quickly around to the backside of the brushy tract of woods, and went in blind, hoping against hope I could find him again. As it worked out, I did find him, and I messed with him until he quit me at the customary 11 a.m. I guess he was a union turkey or something.

Sid and I went crappie fishing on one of the lease's several oxbow lakes that afternoon, and we were in the back yard cleaning the catch for tomorrow's supper when old Crazy gobbled. He wasn't 75 yards across the bayou, directly behind The Camp. This turkey had no discernible pattern.

"You want to double-team him with me in the morning?" I asked.

"Hell, no," Sid said. "I'm not climbing that muddy bank for love nor turkey."

*   *   *

Next morning I was across the bayou and up the bank before dawn even thought about breaking. Crazy sounded off just like he did yesterday, in the black dark and not 50 yards from where we'd heard him just before dark yesterday. I crept close and set up, with him between me and The Camp. I was 60 yards from his tree, and I couldn't resist making a little peep-peep tree call while it was still dark.

I immediately wished I hadn't done it, because he never gobbled again. When the light grew I could see him up there, facing me, looking

145

at trees and ground for that hen he'd heard in the dark. There was a little accidental arena halfway between us, an opening in the brush half the size of a tennis court. It was an inviting landing zone, and it was within gun range. Things would have been looking good except for the fact that he hadn't gobbled since I'd tree called. I figured I'd screwed it up, but there he was and there I was, pinned down like a bug. Nothing to do but sit there and beat myself up.

But it worked out okay. After 45 minutes of silence, the gobbler tipped forward, fell off his limb into a short glide, and landed right in the center of that LZ, 24 yards off my raised gun barrel. I know that because I stepped it off after I shot him. The Crazy Gobbler of Crazy Bayou had proved his craziness again, by pulling a jake stunt even though he had the spurs of a four-year-old.

When Sid got back to The Camp – he never hunted very long, since he hunted every day of the season – Crazy was hanging on the porch, Sid's Bloody Mary was ready, two hard-fried eggs were draining excess grease on a napkin-lined paper plate, and the bacon was sizzling.

Jill J Easton

In the end, the Crazy Gobbler's unpredictability proved his undoing.

Chapter 18

The Boss of the Brake

He roosted in the middle of an ancient river oxbow that had ceased being a lake centuries ago. Now it was what we here in the South call a brake or a slash – a dense stand of cypress and tupelo gum trees growing in shallow, tannin-stained water choked with limbs and downed logs, with a bottom so flocculent you'd sink to your waist in it, assuming you were foolhardy enough to go in there in the first place.

I was young and foolhardy, but not *that* foolhardy. Still, I wanted very badly to shoot the gobbler that was singing the song of his people from one of the trees out there over the black water. The brake was 200, maybe 250 yards wide, and the turkey was pretty much in the middle of it. This was early in my turkey hunting career and I hadn't yet tagged my 10th gobbler, but green as I was, I still knew he could go out either way and I needed to do something to tilt the playing field.

One of my turkey hunting mentors, Tommy Aycock (read about him in Chapter 39 of *Bad Birds 2*,) taught me it's risky to call much to a turkey that's still on the roost, because it will often make him stay in the tree and wait for the hen to show up under him. But Tommy also taught me the no-call rule doesn't apply if the gobbler in question is roosted over water. Turkey hens aren't known for their swimming ability, and turkey gobblers know it.

So I was pouring it on pretty heavy. I'm sure my calling back then was awful, but I thought it sounded great. Apparently, so did the gobbler. He was pouring it on as heavy as I was, and every time he gobbled, it further reinforced my urge to keep calling.

Looking back, I'm pretty sure he would have come to the ground earlier if I'd slacked off enough to give him a chance to clear his head and think about getting on with his morning business, but I kept him in an absolute froth and he stayed out there for a full hour after sunrise. He'd have stayed even longer if it hadn't been for the two silent jakes that finally pitched out from trees near the hot gobbler. They sailed over my head where I sat, ten yards from the edge of the water, and landed 50 feet behind me on the natural levee of slightly higher ground that borders most river oxbows.

That was when I realized I'd set up too close to the edge, leaving no room for a turkey to land in front of me. (I told you I was green.) The *aha!* moment came too late, though. With the two turkeys so close behind me I'd spook them for sure, so I sat tight. Even at my abysmal level of skill and experience, I finally realized I needed to quit calling. The longbeard out in the brake gobbled four or five more times, and then I heard him leave his limb. I picked him out as he sailed through the tree trunks, angling my way. He got over dry land less than 50 yards down the brake from me, but he continued sailing past the low ridge where the jakes had landed. He gobbled when he got on the ground, more than 100 yards behind me.

I'd lost track of the jakes. Or, more accurately, I'd forgotten about them in the excitement of seeing that big longbeard sail past. Whichever, I knew I needed to get turned around if I was going to have any chance at tagging the longbeard. If I could have stayed low and scooted around my tree I might have gotten away with it. But I'd sat against a fallen log instead of a standing tree, and when I stood up to step over it the jakes started clucking and putting. I sat down as fast as I could and started giving them some low, contented stuff, but they'd seen me and the damage was done.

A few minutes later, after the two youngsters had moved off through the woods, still nervously clucking, I called to the longbeard again. He answered, but he was a little farther away than he had been, and each time he gobbled thereafter, he was farther yet. Pretty soon I was all by myself in the green, pretty bottomland woods, contemplating both my belly button and the chain of mistakes I'd committed that morning: sitting too close to the brake, calling too much, spooking the jakes when I turned around.

*   *   *

The next morning I was back beside the brake, determined not to make those mistakes again. When he started gobbling from about the same place out over the water, I moved back to the natural levee and set up about where the jakes had landed the day before. The turkey was gobbling as much today as he had yesterday, but I didn't want to paralyze him again. I gave him one soft set of tree yelps, and when he answered I laid my call down.

That first decision was a good one. Just before sunrise, the two jakes sailed toward me again on pretty much the same glide path, and when they lit they were less than 30 yards away. They had me pinned down but I didn't care. I was confident the gobbler would soon join them.

But my second decision, the one where I didn't call very much, didn't work out so hot. In the absence of any encouragement at all, the gobbler flew on through the brake and went to the ground on the other side. I belatedly started calling to him, but it was too late. He gobbled over there for more than an hour before going quiet. Gobbled up some hens, most likely.

I'd hunted deer, ducks and squirrels around the brake for years, and I knew the woods were thick and brushy on the other side, due

Tommy Aycock

Jim Spencer

to a fairly recent logging operation. But I also knew it would take me more than an hour to get over there with the turkey. With him now gone silent, the odds were stacked long against me. I decided to stay put.

At that early stage of my turkey hunting life, I was still perfectly willing to shoot short-bearded turkeys, but by then the jakes that had landed on me had wandered off. There was another turkey gobbling intermittently in the distance, however, and I hurried to him as fast as I could and set up about 200 yards away.

Everything fell into place. He gobbled hard at my first call. Ditto the second, and he'd cut the distance in half. I didn't call again until I clucked to make him raise his head. Tommy Aycock lived close by, so on my way to the check station I went by to show him my two-year-old trophy. He hadn't come in from hunting yet, but as I was backing out of his driveway he pulled in with a grin on his face and a hook-spurred old warrior in his truck. It wouldn't be the last time he one-upped me.

*   *   *

The next day, armed with Tommy's advice about how to hunt the Boss of the Brake, I was back at my now-familiar listening spot. "If he's out there in the middle, you don't need to set up right away," Tommy said. "Move around a little bit at first. Call to him more than you did yesterday, but don't get carried away like you did the first day. Get him gobbling pretty good, and then slack off on your calling, like you're bored with it. Make him think you're losing interest. Then sit down and shut up. See if that works."

So that's what I did. I tree yelped to him after he started gobbling on his own, and when he answered me I waited a few more minutes and did what I thought was a pretty decent fly-down sequence: yelp a little louder, fly-down cackle and slapping my hat on my leg to imitate wingbeats, a longer run of yelps a few seconds later. He gobbled at my racket and I cut-yelped back at him. He gobbled again; I ran the same sequence. He gobbled again.

I was sucking in air to call again when I remembered Tommy's words. *…don't get stupid about it like you did that first day.* I let the air escape without running it over the mouth call, and it was one of the most difficult exhales of my life.

Remembering Tommy's other advice, I started moving back and forth along the bank of the brake, calling softly every minute or two. Ten minutes of that and I quit calling and set up along the natural levee, a hundred yards south of the roosted gobbler. He gobbled hard for another 15 minutes, then went silent. Twenty more minutes passed. It was starting to look like I'd screwed up again.

Then a flicker of dark movement in the woods caught my eye, and here came the Boss, walking slowly along the levee. I hadn't heard him fly out of the brake, but obviously he had. He took two or three steps and stopped. Looked. Took a few more steps and stopped again.

He caught me with my gun in my lap, and when I first saw him he was already killable. It was obvious he was looking for the hen he'd been talking to, but it was equally obvious he wasn't fully convinced. I was in deep shade, though, with some low bushes in front, so I was able to very slowly raise the gun to a low port position and get the safety disengaged.

He took three more steps and stopped to look. The range was now inside 30 yards. When he took the first of his customary three more steps, I brought the gun smoothly to my shoulder. He caught the movement, but movement was what he'd been looking for. He jerked to a stop and raised his head another six inches, and it gave me all the time I needed.

Several firsts were accomplished with that trigger pull.

It was the first time I killed two turkeys on consecutive days.

It was the first time I killed a gobbler that came in silent.

It was my first gobbler with spurs longer than 1-1/4 inches.

And most important to me then, it was the first time I ever beat Tommy Aycock. He drew a goose-egg that day.

Chapter 19

Trapshy

The late-January morning dawned crisp, bright and windless, a perfect day to do what we were doing: running an extensive predator trapline in the eastern Ozarks where we live. Despite the low fur prices of late, Jill and I still trap for several weeks every winter, partly because we are trappers through and through and partly because turkeys in our part of the world have taken a serious hit. Since predation is one of the things hitting them, it's a win-win: we get to do what we enjoy, and the turkeys benefit from a reduced predator population.

We weren't quite a third of the way through our line, and it had already been a productive run. Two bobcats and two coons were cooling in the bed of the truck. The next set location was one of our best, a saddle in a low ridge connecting two mountains. Gentle, shallow valleys sloped away on each side of the saddle, and a seldom-used two track traversed it lengthwise. ATV trails came up out of each valley and met on the main road. It was the intersection of several travelways, a perfect set location, and our hopes were high as we drove toward it.

But it was a downer this morning. When we topped the last little rise and the set location scrolled into view, the commotion that greeted us wasn't what we wanted to see. Jill's set, where she'd caught a gray fox two days before, was empty. My set, 30 yards past hers, held a wildly flopping adult turkey gobbler. It doesn't happen often, but it happens.

Releasing a 20-pound gobbler from a trap is an adventure. Your objective is to release the bird quickly but without further harm to either the bird or to yourself, and both things are eminently possible. It's almost a given that the turkey already has a broken toe, and your goal here is to set him free before the broken toe escalates into a broken leg. To do this safely (gobblers have spurs, remember?) you have to get the bird under control. Over the years I've released five turkeys, and the best way I've found to do it is by covering the bird's head and wrapping my arms around its body before depressing the trap springs with my feet.

I threw my jacket over the gobbler's head and got him in a bear hug. When the trap was off his foot, Jill examined him for damage. "His toe is pretty badly broken," she said. "Nothing holding it but a couple tendons."

We decided to amputate the toe (inside toe, left foot) before releasing the turkey, and while I held him tight Jill performed the operation. "Really nice spurs," she said. "Looks like he was a three-year-old last spring."

I set the turkey down and snatched my jacket off his head. He lost no time getting out of there; two steps and he was airborne, two seconds and he was flying 40 miles per hour and accelerating. He sailed out of the saddle and disappeared down the east valley, flying like his life depended on it. He probably thought it did.

*   *   *

Now it's April, and we're turkey hunting along that same two-track road. On foot this time. We used the little rise before the saddle as our listening spot that morning, and when gobbling time came we heard one farther down the road, maybe 100 yards past the trail intersection where I'd caught the gobbler.

He was roosted off the two-track but not far, and it seemed like the best option was to move down to our end of the saddle and set up there. That would put us within 150 yards of the bird, give or take a few, and would give him an unobstructed pathway straight to our calling.

It was a nice battle plan, but it failed anyway. The gobbler flew down but stayed on his side of the saddle, answering our calls and sounding eager but refusing to come across. The saddle was too open for us to advance on him along the road, so we dropped off the right side, got far enough downslope to have cover, and moved past both the saddle and the gobbler. When we were 200 yards past him we climbed back up to the road. We were just getting our new set finalized when I heard a hen yelping in the valley we'd just left. I called to her, trying to get her headed my way, but she went straight to the gobbler. He dummied up, and that was the end of our business with him that day.

*   *   *

Jill wanted to check another place the next morning, and I went back to the two-track alone. Dawn came cloudy and windy, and I heard nothing in the vicinity of the saddle. After standing around until well past fly-down time, I went through the saddle and walked another mile on the road, to where it ended at a circle turnaround-slash-log yard. It was nearly noon when I came back along the road, working my way to the truck and calling as I went. It was still cloudy and windy, and now it was starting to look like rain.

Just before I dropped into the saddle it started. Not hard, but rain nonetheless. Great. Like all other turkey hunters, I just loooove hunting them in the rain. But here I was, more than a mile from the truck, so I stopped and called. A turkey answered me from the other side of the saddle. It sounded like he was on the road and on the rise where I'd listened at dawn. I dropped down the slope until I was on the saddle and set up 40 yards shy of where I'd caught the gobbler in January. He gobbled back when I called. The rain got harder. It got

157

Jill J Easton

This big male bobcat came along the night after we released Trapshy. Good thing he didn't come a night earlier, or this Bad Birds chapter would have never happened.

darker. A minute or two later I saw him coming along the road. Okay, good. I was getting wet, but I was fixing to kill the gobbler.

The turkey was 60 yards from me and still walking steadily my way. I had my gun up. My safety was showing red. At 45 yards I thought about shooting him but decided to wait. Thirty-yard turkeys are better than 45-yard turkeys, and this one showed every indication of becoming a 30-yard turkey. He was still 40 yards out, at the exact spot where I'd caught the turkey three months before, when another gobble came from the rise on the other side of the saddle. The turkey stopped and turned to look back along the road. The licorice-stick stub sticking out of his chest brought my finger off the trigger.

The still unseen gobbler sounded off again, and the young bird resumed his walk down my gun barrel. I held still and let him do it. I was five feet off the road, and he walked past me without a pause. I returned my attention to the road. The turkey down that way gobbled again. I called. He gobbled again. The first rumble of thunder came out of the clouds. He gobbled at that. It rained harder.

I called. He gobbled. It thundered. He gobbled. And then, brothers and sisters, the bottom fell out. Between one second and the next, what had been a moderate shower turned into a Biblical downpour. In the space of five seconds I went from damp to drenched, and my enjoyment index fell from barely okay to not even a little bit.

I had been in this situation before. If you are working a strong-gobbling turkey when a sudden deluge shuts the hunt down, you can usually kill that bird by walking swiftly toward where the last gobble came from. You'll often find the turkey hunkered in place, looking miserable and waiting for the downpour to end. I tested the strategy again this time, and sure enough, I walked right up on him. He was inside 30 yards when I first picked him out, and I could have killed him easily. But I didn't want to kill him that way. Instead, I kept walking straight at him, curious to see just how close I could get.

I have no way of knowing if this is typical or not, but I got within ten feet of that gobbler before he roused himself and ran away. I continued my soggy way back to the truck smiling in the rain. This turkey was mine. Whether I ever killed him or not, I had now counted coup.

*   *   *

It rained for the rest of that day and well into the night, and I didn't hunt the next morning because thunder was still rumbling and radar showed more rain coming. It was past nine before things lined out, and I waited until ten before going to the woods so some of the post-storm drippage would be over with.

He was gobbling when I got to the rise above the saddle, and again he was on the other side of it. Same result as before – he refused to come to me across the saddle, and I dropped into the valley and got past him, then came back up to the road and tried to call him in from there.

Today, though, there was no busybody hen to come along and mess things up. He gobbled eagerly at my first yelps, and less than ten minutes after I sat to him I tipped him over at 25 yards. I stood up, watched him for a minute to make sure he was fully dead, then gathered up my stuff and walked to where he lay in the two-track. I went through my normal ritual. I laid my hand on his warm body and thanked him, I rolled him partway over to check his beard, then onto his back to check his spurs.

The results of my ritual were that the gobbler had a warm, smooth body, he did not say "You're welcome" when I thanked him, he had a beard like a whisk broom, and his spurs were magnificent.

And one more thing: he was missing the inside toe on his left foot.

He wasn't a Bad Bird at all. He was just trapshy.

Chapter 20

The Horse Farm Gobblers

We were in Maine, Randy Northern and me, on the last half of a turkey odyssey. I'd killed a gobbler two days earlier (see Chapter 13) but so far Randy hadn't had any luck and he was needing a turkey. With four days left in the season, we moved farther south in the state and found a horse boarding/horse training ranch that showed promise.

Shifting our base of operations used up most of the day, and we only had time for a short evening hunt. Still, it gave us a feel for the potential of this new place. Randy went west from the ranch headquarters while I crossed a pretty trout stream and headed east. Neither of us saw turkeys, but I found lots of sign and heard several distant gobbles. Randy heard several heavy birds fly up at sundown. We felt good about the morning hunt.

At first light I was in the vicinity of the gobbling I'd heard, and the turkeys – four of them, I think – started tearing the woods down. Two weren't all that vocal, but the other two were in rare form. For more than two hours they didn't let five seconds pass without one or the other sounding off. Usually both. I heard an entire season's worth of gobbling in that one two-hour span.

During that noisy period, I changed sets six times with nothing to show for it. As far as I could tell, they never moved more than a few yards in any direction. I switched calls as often as I switched set-ups, but they gobbled so much I couldn't tell if they were answering me or not.

On my seventh move, I bumped an outlying hen. She didn't panic but she got nervous, and her jittery clucking broke the stalemate. The two talkative gobblers started angling away from me. They didn't stop gobbling, but they fell back into a less frenetic pattern. I listened to them leave, then started toward where I'd heard a few distant gobbles during the two-hour gobble-athon.

I got on the other gobbler easily enough, but he was henny and declined my invitation. Nine o'clock found me moving and calling, still prospecting for a biddable turkey. I made a big loop and by 10 was circling back toward the horse barn when I came across a logging trace not far from where I'd lost track of the talkative gobblers two hours before.

For probably the ten thousandth time in my hunting career, I made the mistake of calling without first locating a suitable set-up tree. For probably the five hundredth time, my mistake bit me in the butt. When I hit that old box call, a turkey answered from so close I could hear the breathy rattle in the bottom of his gobble. Half a second later, his buddy chimed in. I fell down beside the nearest tree, no mask, no gloves, and I didn't even have time to get my gun up before they stepped into sight at 25 yards.

Through some quirk of fate they didn't see me, and after a few seconds of intent staring in my direction they both moved to my left and went behind some greenery. That gave me a chance to shoulder the gun. I was ready when they stepped out again, but I couldn't shoot because both heads were lined up and I'd already used one of my Maine tags. They continued to move slowly to the left, their heads maddeningly glued together. It was one of the most frustrating minutes I've ever spent as a turkey hunter. They went behind some more green stuff, gobbled again, and that was the end of the encounter. Ten minutes later I eased the gun back to my lap, leaned my head back against the four-inch sapling I was sitting on, and said a word I didn't learn from my mother.

*   *   *

The next morning I was standing exactly where the two gobblers had started the day before, and I found out why they didn't want to leave it. It was a deer hunter's mini-food plot, a 30-yard circle of tender green grass and clover complete with ten-foot-high stand, at the convergence of five old roads and ATV trails – a perfect strutting stage for a longbeard to show his stuff. In anticipation of a repeat performance, I stuck a few bushes and made a blind on the east side of the opening and settled in to wait for the dynamic duo to make their appearance.

They started gobbling pretty much on schedule, not as much as yesterday but still quite a bit, and they were close enough to my set-up to give me confidence. I didn't call until they were on the ground, and when I did, they cut me off. A few minutes later, it was evident they were heading my way. I called once more just to seal the deal. They answered, and I laid the call down and got the gun on my knee.

They came to me on a string, and when they gobbled at 75 yards I adjusted my barrel direction a few degrees and got my cheek down on the stock. They gobbled again at 60 yards, and I fine-tuned my aiming point. Show time.

That's when everything went sideways. Just a few seconds after the 60-yard gobble, both gobblers went into a stutter-clucking frenzy and blew out over the food plot like two crop-dusters climbing out of a run over a cotton field. One flew straight over me and the other flared to my right. I tracked the overhead gobbler with my gun barrel, swinging through the target like I've done on mallards time and again.

The only thing I omitted was pulling the trigger. It's a lesson I've learned the hard way over nearly a half-century of being bested by gobblers: shooting flying turkeys is a good way to cripple them. I'm still a little proud of myself for my restraint this time. And I never did find out what spooked the gobblers, but my guess is coyote or bobcat.

Whatever, it put an end to my doing anything with those two gobblers that day. I gave them an hour to calm down, but wasn't able to reconnect, so I hunted elsewhere the rest of the day.

*   *   *

Meanwhile, Randy had been dueling with his own pair of longbeards on the other side of the horse farm, with no more luck than I'd been having. In the motel that night we briefly considered swapping opponents for the third day, but decided against it because we'd both worked up a good mad-on at the turkeys and didn't want to share them with anybody.

Soooo, morning three found me back near the deer stand/food plot. The stubborn, talkative pair cranked up right on schedule, but they were in a different direction this time. I had a quiet, easy, quick approach along a low ridge that paralleled the trout stream. OnX threw me a curve, though. It was supposed to be unbroken woods between my position and a paved road 800 yards away, but the closer I got to the turkeys, the more I sensed something was out of whack. Chickens were clucking from where the gobblers were gobbling. Never a good sign.

Sure enough, the woods in front of me started opening up, and I found myself looking across the creek at the back side of a fine, new house sitting in a two-acre partially cleared yard, complete with a trampoline, an above-ground swimming pool and one of those multi-colored plastic slide/tunnel/swing/monkey bar combination gym sets that kids never play on. The gobblers were in a tree in the back yard.

Figuring it would be tacky to shoot a gobbler in somebody's yard, I retreated 200 yards and when I was sure I was back on the horse farm I set up and started calling. Wonder of wonders, the gobblers

Jim Spencer

At least one of us could hit something that day.

eagerly responded, and not long afterward they were on the ground and headed my way. They were still on the other side of the creek, but it wasn't a big creek and I was in a position to shoot across it if necessary.

And it was. They came side by side along the far side of the creek, and when they broke the perimeter of the magic 40-yard circle I squeezed the trigger on the right-hand bird, the closer of the two by three or four yards.

How in the world I missed him is a mystery for the ages, but miss him I did, and I missed him again with the second barrel as he and his buddy turned to skedaddle. Adding insult to injury, they ran 40 yards into the horse pasture and stopped, now well out of range. They spent the next two minutes clucking back and forth, trying to figure out what had just happened.

During that two minutes I sent Randy a text: "Missed twice." He responded immediately: "Nooooo!!!" I was still watching the two puzzled gobblers in the pasture when Randy's 12 gauge boomed twice, and a minute or two later my text alert buzzed again: It showed two strutting turkey emojis. My buddy had made up for my miscue, in spades.

We still had one day left to hunt, but Randy had filled his tags and I'd blown my chance and didn't deserve another. We were on the road within the hour and in Scranton, Pennsylvania by sundown.

Chapter 21

Smokey

"The year's at the spring
And day's at the morn;
Morning's at seven;
The hillside's dew-pearled;
The lark's on the wing;
The snail's on the thorn
God's in his Heaven —
All's right with the world!"

Well, morning comes a bit earlier than seven in the turkey woods, but since Robert Browning wasn't a turkey hunter, we can forgive his mistake. But thanks to a misspent semester when I thought I wanted to be an English Literature major, that's the verse that was running through my head as I walked the long, U-shaped ridge that carried me away from the well-traveled U.S. Forest Service road and deep into the timber.

For a couple weeks before the season I'd been listening to more than a half-dozen turkeys gobbling in a big valley not far from my house, and I had a couple of them nailed down. They liked to roost off the end of the ridge I was walking, where it toes off into a deep, steep-sided valley. They were easily hearable from the road, but that was because the ridge hooked around the head of another deep, rough hollow that flanked the road. They were about a half-mile from the road with nothing but air between, but to reach them you had to either cross that deep canyon or walk more than two miles around the curve of the ridge.

Well before first light on Opening Day, I'd already walked that ridge and was in there with them. Roosted ain't roasted, as Cuz Strickland famously said, but I'd walked that same U-shaped ridge and put these two birds to bed the previous evening, and I knew exactly where they were sleeping. I also knew where they'd flown up from and where they liked to go after they flew down. Because of the degree of difficulty in reaching them, I didn't think I'd have any company. I figured my chances were pretty good, which explains Browning's verse from *Pippa's Song* running through my head.

The big woods are quiet during that lull before shift change. The coons, bobcats and other night prowlers are winding down their workday, and the day-shift critters are just beginning to stretch. I was waiting for the first cardinal and the following first gobble when that dawn silence was broken by the sound of gravel crunching under vehicle tires across the canyon on the road. Not just a truck or two. Multiple vehicles, a convoy of them, several of them heavy diesel rigs, and they stopped directly across the canyon from me. Then truck doors started slamming, and voices – many voices – came at me across the canyon. Loud voices, arguing, laughing, barking orders.

About then my turkeys started gobbling, and plain as day I heard one of the voices remark on it: "I bet those gobblers won't like all this smoke."

That's when I understood. What I was hearing was a Forest Service fire crew, and they were getting ready to start a controlled burn. *On the Opening Day of turkey season.* I am not kidding you. Opening Day.

Don't misunderstand me here; I'm no tree-hugger. As a trained forester and wildlife biologist (I came to my senses and walked away from that English Lit stuff,) I understand the need for controlled burns, from both the forestry and wildlife sides of the issue. And as a landowner who lives on a small inholding completely surrounded by national forest, I'm glad the powers that be have an active burning program here. But there are times to leave the drip torches in the tool shed, and the first day of spring turkey season is one of those times. I know our national forests are designated as multiple-use properties, but come on.

I'm a bit of a hothead, especially when it comes to unwarranted interference on a turkey hunt, and my first impulse was to march back out of there and raise hell at everybody in sight. Maybe shoot out a truck tire or two. But the two turkeys I was after were still gobbling lustily and the urge quickly passed – or at least got postponed.

The gobblers didn't seem bothered by the noise, nor by the smoke that soon started drifting through the woods around me. They flew down, messed around a while, then came strutting in side by side. They broke the 40-yard circle and I let them come another 10 yards, then killed the closest one when he stuck his head up in response to my soft cluck. Then I watched for a few minutes as the thick-bearded survivor thrashed and spurred his stricken buddy. Still, though, I was miffed, and the shouts from the fire line hotshots and the sounds of machinery clanking up and down the road did little to help my enjoyment of the moment.

I had heated words with the fire crew chief when I got back to the road. In no uncertain terms, I gave him my opinion about the piss-poor timing of the burn, but I knew all the while I was yelling at the wrong person. My real beef was with the District Ranger, but of course he was nowhere to be seen. (I did, however, catch up to him later that spring, and his ears are still burning.)

*   *   *

Timing notwithstanding, it was a good burn – fast-moving with the gentle breeze, the forest floor dry enough to carry a ground litter fire but not dry enough to let anything get too hot. The next morning, with the pressure off and a tag still in my pocket, I decided to go back to the fresh burn to see how the turkeys reacted to the disturbance. But rather than making the long hike down the ridge, I listened from the road.

It was hard for me to believe then, and it's almost as hard now, but where I'd been hearing six gobblers before the season and before the burn, that morning I heard fourteen. And remember, I'd already killed one of the original six. Every one of the gobblers I heard that day was in the still-smoking controlled burn area. Not one across the road in the unburned forest. I wasn't ignorant of the attraction a new burn has for turkeys – crispy critters, exposed acorns, tender new growth and all that – but for it to happen this fast?

It was a thing to ponder, but the pondering could come later. Right now there were turkeys to hunt, and lots of them. It was a long way to go, but because I already had this gobbler patterned and I'd seen him flog my turkey yesterday and knew he was a good one, I went after the bird on the end of the long ridge. He was on the ground long before I got to him, but he was still gobbling a lot, so I had no trouble keeping track of him and getting in close. The trouble started when I called to him.

I'd hunted turkeys in burns before, but I'd never hunted them in a burn so fresh I had to watch out where I sat for fear of burning my bottom. That's exactly what happened at my first set. It was fine at first, but as the gobbler began to circle to the right as I worked him, I shifted around my tree to stay in position to shoot…and scooted directly onto a branch with a live coal still in it. I got off it quick, but not quick enough. My wife says I still have a pink scar back there.

Evidently I also didn't get off that clinker quietly enough, because I never heard the gobbler again after the hotseat episode. I guess he'd been closer than I thought. Or maybe I squealed louder than I thought. Whichever, it ended the hunt, and I went home to get patched up.

A slight aside here: She who tells me I have a scar on my ass, she who rendered the first aid that day, is not a Florence Nightingale. There's nothing wrong with her nursing skills, but her bedside manner leaves a lot to be desired. My wound was not nearly as funny as she obviously thought it was, and her lack of sympathy was not ameliorated by the fact that she'd killed a big gobbler that morning.

*   *   *

Anyway…the next morning, Betadined and Band-Aid butted, I was in the burn again. This time I committed to the ridge well before daylight. I wanted to be with the gobbler when he woke up. Smoke was still drifting around in the burn; lots of rich pine stumps were still smoldering, and here and there a log or stump was still actively burning. Easing through the dark, smoky woods, I thought about my grandfather, moving through the Argonne Forest in the closing days of World War I. It was a spooky sensation, and I wasn't even being shot at. There was little wind, none really, and the smoke lay heavy on the ground.

But my turkey cranked up at first light, smoky woods and all. He'd picked up what sounded like a pair of jakes, and they were attempting to gobble along with him. One of them had just about mastered his grown-up voice, but the other's attempts sounded more like croaks than gobbles. After a polite period of roost gobbling and croaking, the three turkeys flew down. I saw one of them in the air but have no idea which one it was. I waited until the big boy gobbled from the ground and then I hit him with a fast cut/yelp and immediately got up. Using the smoke to hide me, I moved sideways 30 yards, not wanting to gain ground on the turkey, just wanting to change my position a little.

As soon as I called from my new spot, the gobbler answered, and he'd also moved. Now he was closer, I judged not more than 75 yards off the gun. The smoke was thick but at that range I was hesitant to move again. It was a wise decision. Twenty seconds later he gobbled again, and then I heard him drumming. If I can hear that, he's a killable turkey if I can see him. Trouble was, I couldn't.

Visibility was terrible. First, it was a cloudy day, and it was still very early. Second, the ground, the lower part of the tree trunks and the gobbler were all black. And finally there was the drifting smoke. The drumming intensified, and in this claustrophobic atmosphere, the already ventriloquistic sound seemed like it was coming from every direction, even above and below. And it was getting louder.

Ffffttt-dooooommm. Ffffttt-dooooommm.

I was about to wear my eyeball muscles out, looking around for the gobbler. He was nowhere to be found. Then the sound started fading, and before it disappeared altogether I figured I ought to call. When I did, he gobbled directly behind me from maybe 40 yards away. That was why I hadn't seen him. I didn't have eyes in the back of my head. I took a chance, hoping the smoke and poor visibility would hide me, and leaned around my tree to see if I could get a shot.

Nothing. Just black tree trunks, black ground, and smoke. I called again. The answering gobble came from 80 yards away. I'd lost him. He was going off the ridge into the canyon that lay between ridge and road. I tried to flank him and go downhill with him, but the farther down the slope we went the more the smoke thinned. When it got too thin to help hide my movements in the open woods, I gave up. He was traveling faster than I was, anyway.

And my butt was killing me.

*   *   *

I only had one more day to hunt before leaving for an extended road trip. There were lots of other turkeys I could have gone to that last morning, but my reasoning went like this:

--You've already killed an Arkansas turkey, so the pressure is off.

--This turkey you're hunting is a good one, you've already seen him.

--You more or less know his habits and travel pattern, and you don't have that edge with any of these other birds you're hearing.

--And this smokey bird has caused you a grievous buttockular wound and needs to pay for it.

At that point, I realized I'd just named this turkey. Given all that, how could I not give him one last chance to die?

So guess where I was the fourth (and my last) morning of my home season?

Smokey and his jakes woke up about normal time, and I was there to hear them. The smoke wasn't as bad, but it still wasn't what you'd call good air quality on that ridge. Sort of like hunting in a thin fog – things were a little out of focus at a distance, but for the most part clear inside shotgun range. The gobbler trio were a little farther down the slope of the ridge than they'd been before, and I was able to get closer and set up within the perimeter of their usual landing zone. I figured that even if they were too far downhill to sail all the way to this happy place, there was a good chance they'd come to it – especially if a hen was making sweet talk up here.

My hopes kicked up a notch when two hens started yelping in trees behind me as daylight invaded the blackened woods. The gobblers answered them, and shortly the hens flew down right behind me. I waited, and when one of them walked into my peripheral vision on her way to the gobblers, I spooked her with a wave of my arm, and she putted as she took off running.

I immediately started mimicking her, and as she faded from hearing I slowly calmed down the intensity and volume of my own calling, finally finishing it off with a trio of soft, contented yelps.

Smokey hadn't made a peep during all that racket, and I held my breath when I finished. After 30 seconds I slowly let the breath out and shook my head. On the second shake, Smokey gobbled. He was coming up the hill; it had worked.

I felt like a riverboat gambler with a Mississippi flush (that's a small handgun and any five cards.) I didn't know if what I'd done with the hen would be enough to close the deal, but unless somebody showed up with a lot more firepower, I was fixing to win this hand.

I saw him at 80 yards but couldn't make sure it was him until I saw him again at 60. He was slipping, using the series of blackened tree trunks between us to hide his forward progress. I snugged the black 870 to my shoulder and waited.

I saw him once more at 50 yards. Then I didn't see him any more. Five excruciating minutes passed. I was scanning the woods in a 90-degree arc, certain he'd be in range next time I saw him, knowing in my heart he was there already.

When he gobbled off my right ear he was within 15 yards. I cut my eyes hard that way. He'd seen me flinch and was already halfway out of strut, and though I knew better my adrenaline-lubed nerves betrayed me. Instead of smoothly making the move – a long shot at best – I took the odds from long to astronomical by jerking the barrel to the right and trying to get the bead on his head. I had no chance.

He was in motion as soon as I was, and he was behind a tree before I could bring the gun to bear. He got away without drawing fire, and I got up, coughed up some black gunk, carefully wiped some of the soot off my still-tender butt, and went home to pack.

Chapter 22

The Junkman's Spawn

It was a week into turkey season and I was riding high. The day before, I'd tagged a particularly nasty gobbler that had his story told in *Bad Birds 2*. I hadn't scouted the place this spring, but I knew it well from a decade of spring hunts there. I knew it would hold turkeys if anyplace did. I also knew where to start looking.

I parked at the familiar log yard and stood listening beside the truck, fully expecting to hear a gobbler sound off nearby. The old yard looked somewhat different than it had the first time I parked there. For one thing, the trees reclaiming the opening were considerably bigger than they'd been 15 years earlier. But the main difference was that the Forest Service, or somebody with their head on straight, had cleaned up the old junkpile that once sat beside the yard, big as Jabba the Hutt and twice as ugly. The first time she saw it, Jill had referred to the tangle of household refuse as "a junkman's toy box." (See Chapter 2 for that story.)

But the woods surrounding the log yard looked the same – big shortleaf pines on the high ground to the left, a pretty hardwood bottom falling gently away to the right. And when the first turkey gobbled five minutes after I shut off the truck, he was very close to where I thought he'd be – out in the bottom, 250 yards away and southwest of me.

I already had my vest on. I grabbed the 28 gauge and hustled west, back along the two-track I'd driven in on. I needed to get on the other side of this gobbler before setting up, and it was going to take some time. When I'd gone far enough to be well past him, I entered the hardwood bottom and crossed it until I hit another stand of pines on the other side. Where the ground rose and the timber type changed is where I made my set, so I could cover both the high and low ground. I was 150 yards from the turkey. I'd wanted to get closer, but the woods in there were open and dry and I didn't want to take a chance on getting heard or seen. Daylight was growing fast.

He was still gobbling and still in the tree when I got everything ready. So far I hadn't heard any hen talk, but I was expecting some. They didn't disappoint, but they did surprise. The first tree yelp came from, of all places, the tree against which I'd made my set. She was answered by several other hens, all within shotgun range.

It was a bad development. The gobbler was too close for me to try to scatter the hens; he'd see me for sure. But there was still plenty of room for the hens to fly down between him and me and cut me off. That is, unless they looked down and picked me out before flying down. I didn't want them to screw up the hunt by spooking and making a bunch of scared turkey sounds, so I figured my best option was to hold absolutely still and do absolutely nothing. Of all the many skills required of a turkey hunter, those may be the two I am worst at.

I don't know why those hens stayed up as long as they did. All I know is, it was a long 45 minutes. They yelped contentedly to each other, ignoring the steady, insistent gobbling of the longbeard farther up the bottom. Somehow, I resisted the near-constant urge to raise my head and look at them in the trees. When they finally did fly down, they surprised me again by flying not toward the gobbler as I figured, but at a 90-degree angle to his tree, out into the pines on the higher ground.

Their decision evidently surprised the gobbler, too. He gobbled three times while the hens were still in the air, and they'd barely touched down when I heard him take wing, too. A second later I saw him sailing through the pines toward the hens. He never gobbled again after he got on the ground, but I could see him out there strutting and trying to gain control of the situation.

But girls rule, in humans and turkeys alike, and in the end he fell in behind and followed the hens as they drifted south through the big open piney woods. Another bad development. There was almost no understory, and if I wanted to follow them I'd have to be at least 200 yards behind and probably 250 or more. With him not gobbling, that would be nearly impossible.

Another skill required of a turkey hunter is the ability to know when to fold 'em. I'm pretty good at that one. I sat there until the turkeys were good and gone, then gave it another 15 minutes and checked him with a loud run of cuts on my box. He did not answer.

I folded 'em.

*   *   *

The next morning I approached the hardwood bottom from the south. Coming in that way made for a much longer walk, more than a mile, so I left the house 30 minutes earlier. But the going was easy through the open woods and I made better time than I figured. It was still full-on dark when I stopped 200 yards short of the bottom and sat on a log to wait for daylight.

The owls began before the day did. It was a mated pair, and they started their duet a half-mile apart back to the south. I've just about quit owling at public-land turkeys because they hear so much of it, but I'm still pretty good at it, and these two were having such a good conversation I couldn't resist butting in. When I let out with that long scream you hear sometimes from a fired-up barred owl, there was a long pause as the pair processed the information. The next time they hooted, both were considerably closer to each other and to me. I gave them a short, four-note *who-cooks-for-you?* hoot, and they came closer. Pretty soon they were above me, hooting angrily almost nonstop, and I let well enough alone and gave them the stage.

It was more than the gobbler could stand. He ripped off an angry gobble, then another and another, not quick enough to qualify as a triple gobble, but not far off the mark. The owls never shut up, and a few seconds later he gobbled again. By that time I was on my feet and headed his way. The sky was turning gray over there where it was supposed to, but it was still plenty dark enough for me to crowd him a little. That was desirable with this turkey because of his hens; the closer I could get, the less chance they'd cut me off.

I set up less than 50 yards from his tree. That's closer than I usually like to be, but in this case I made an exception because of the – well, you know. I leaned against my tree, happy as a mink at a minnow farm, and listened to the owls still raising hell and the gobbler still raising it right back.

When the little flock of "well, you know" birds started adding their tree calls to the morning cacophony, I got even happier. They were 75 to 100 yards behind me. Things were looking up.

An interesting thing happened, though, when the hens started talking. When the gobbler heard them, his interest switched instantly from making war to making love, and there was a subtle but definite change in the tone and timbre of his gobbling. I've heard thousands of turkeys gobble, but this was a new experience for me. I can't describe the change for you, but I picked up on it. The passion in his gobble was still there but the anger was gone, replaced by something less warlike and more seductive. Maybe it was because I was so close to the gobbler I could hear things that would be inaudible at distance. I don't know. But it was real, and I heard it.

Anyway, beside the point. The sky got brighter and I picked the gobbler out in the tree, He was close to the trunk, unusual for a big gobbler in my experience, and facing me. More accurately, facing the hens. I will confess to you here: for a few minutes I thought about rolling him off that limb and making up the biggest whopper ever told. But I'd gone more than 40 years without limb-swatting one, and today that total stands at 45.

The owls lost interest in their inter-species quarrel and went away to wherever owls go in daylight, but the gobbler and hens continued their conversation. I didn't feel safe calling to him, because I'd already pushed my luck by crowding him so much. At this range, I didn't want to draw attention to myself. Let him keep looking past me toward the hens, that was fine with me.

My catbird seat situation didn't pan out, though. The hens got more and more talky and finally flew down. It sounded like they were within gun range behind me. I already had my gun on my knee, waiting for the gobbler to come down, but when he did he sailed right by me at a range of ten feet. I guess I could have shot him like a duck coming into the decoys, but I've never done that either, and when he landed he was for sure within gun range. I'm thinking 15 yards, maybe closer.

Even though I was painfully aware he was so close, when he gobbled I flinched. My tree was wide enough to hide the movement, but not the sound when the gun slid off my knee and the barrel hit the ground. The dreaded *putt!* sounds started up behind me, like popcorn starting to pop, and the whole flock moved quickly away. All I could do was sit there and mentally kick my own butt.

I let them go, then took rounders and tried to get back into the bottom ahead of them. I was short, or long, or wide, or something. Whatever, I missed them, and I never made contact again. At about eleven o'clock I folded my hand for the second straight day. On the long walk back to the truck, I gave him his name. It had been 15 years since I'd killed the Junkman, but this gobbler was every bit as ornery. He had to have the same bloodline. *The Junkman's Spawn.*

*   *   *

I'd already hunted hard for nine consecutive days, and I'm not ashamed to admit to a sense of relief when the sound of heavy rain and crashing thunder woke me ahead of the alarm the tenth morning. Several years later, I can still remember the wonderful feeling of flicking the alarm switch off and burrowing back under the covers. I don't specifically remember grinning, but that's the way I'd bet.

When I woke again at 7:15 it was still raining. The downpour continued until sundown, nearly four inches total according to the weatherman. We needed rain but not that much of it, but still it relieved me of having to feel guilty about taking the day off. Yes, I know, you can kill turkeys in the rain, too, and I've done it and written about it. Which is precisely how I know it's not a whole lot of fun.

As expected, things were squishy when I drove into the Junkman's territory on the 11th morning of the season. Two-wheel drive couldn't have handled the job, and even with 4wd I stopped short of where I would have parked in dryer conditions. The rain had moved on and the stars were bright, and after slipping and sliding part of the way in, I parked and walked the rest of the way to the old log yard. No surprise, there was six inches of water standing in the hardwood bottom. I knew the turkeys would roost over that water but they wouldn't fly down into it, so I waded as quietly as possible across to the pines on the other side. I sat down on the higher ground and waited to see where he was roosted today.

I'm still waiting. The old-timers used to say a wet turkey wouldn't gobble. I later learned they were wrong, but if The Junkman's Spawn did it that morning he had moved to a new neighborhood. After gobbling time and fly-down time came and went, I set up and did some blind calling, moving two or three times over the next two hours. I called up a lonesome, bewildered-looking hen, but if The Spawn heard me he didn't do anything about it. At eight-something I went back to my mud-caked truck and hunted elsewhere until noonish, with no more action than I'd have found hunting turkeys in the Astrodome.

*   *   *

Time was running out for home-field hunting. The Arkansas season still had ten days to run, but we were leaving for Indiana in three. I considered abandoning this aggravating Junkman quest and looking elsewhere for a more biddable turkey, but my stubborn streak often overpowers my better judgement. That's how it was this time, and on the 12th day of the season I went to hunt J.S. for the fourth time.

The day dawned muggy, wet and foggy. Not the best beginning for a successful turkey hunt. The bottom had lost most of its standing water, just puddles here and there, but it was still a quagmire. I took a half-dozen steps and gave up. I drove around to the south side, electing to take the long walk through the relatively dry pines rather than fight the mud. That ate up 15 minutes, and the mile-long walk ate up another 20, and J.S. was already on the ground and gobbling hard when I got where I needed to be.

This was a new development. Before, he'd always quit gobbling when he hit the ground with his hens. Maybe he was by himself this morning. I called him and he answered fast. He did the same thing three minutes later, but he hadn't come any closer.

Eighty minutes and two moves later, he still hadn't. I moved one more time, trying to get a little closer, and I guess I bumped him because I never heard him after that. I stayed around in there until the middle of the day without anything to show for it.

*   *   *

I *really* considered going somewhere else – anywhere else – that last day at home. But once again, stubborn trumped smart. Same stuff, different day. He gobbled well on the roost again. The absent hens showed up again. They cut me off again. They led him away again. I followed again. I couldn't catch up again. Blahblahblah. At nine I'd had enough. Again. There was still some packing to do and we had to load the truck. The Junkman's Spawn was safe from me. Not that he hadn't been all along.

We left the house a little before sunrise the next morning, and our route to Indiana took us by the turnoff to where the Junkman's Spawn lived. I asked Jill, "You want to hear a turkey?" She nodded. It was only a three-mile detour.

We pulled into the log yard just as the sun put its first low rays through the pine plantation. I shut off the truck and pushed the button to roll the windows down. They weren't quite all the way down when he gobbled, 250 yards away in the bottom. I honked the horn. He gobbled again.

"There," I said, turning the ignition key. "Now, let's go to Indiana."

Chapter 23

Gobbler 80

According to my turkey log book, it was Friday, April 24, 1992 when I walked into the shop at the Lohman Game Call Company in Neosho, Missouri. Escorting me was Brad Harris, the face and voice of the company during those heyday years. It was after quitting time and the shop was still and quiet. Motes of hardwood dust floated here and there where sunlight slanted through the windows.

I was in Neosho to hook up with Brad and drive to Camdenton for a media turkey hunt. He wanted to give me another Lohman Model 870 box call to replace the one I'd stupidly left beside a tree somewhere in the middle of a wilderness area in south Missouri. Brad walked to a big worktable that must have had 500 box calls on it. He picked three at random and gave each call an experimental run: yelp, cluck, fly-down cackle, cut. He set one call aside, returned the other two to the table and reached for three more. He ran them, laid all three down. Reached for three more.

In less than five minutes he had three calls in his little "keeper" pile. Every call he picked up sounded like a winner to me, but that's what happens when you're listening to a Grand Nationals finalist. He ran each of the three calls again, then handed me one.

"There are lots of turkeys in this call," he said. "Drag 'em out of there."

*　　*　　*

Brad was right, there were lots of turkeys in that call, and over the years I "dragged 'em out of there" at a pretty good clip. The first one I dragged out, matter of fact, was only four days later, at the above-mentioned Lohman media hunt. (See Chapter 24, The Phantom, for the story of that particular Bad Bird.)

That Lohman box went with me on every hunt thereafter, accumulating scratches, stains and intentionally-carved notches, and for 15 years, until I wore the sounding board down flat and it quit sounding good, it was the call I led off with. When I was the guest of a competing call maker – a frequent happening in those days – it stayed hidden in the cargo pocket of my ratty old turkey vest. But it was there, and it was comforting merely because of its presence. Maybe that's silly, but it's no less true because of its silliness.

*　　*　　*

Fast forward to 2007. I'm hunting one of my favorite public places – the Homochitto National Forest in southwest Mississippi. As far as I've been able to determine, there are no easy gobblers on the Homochitto – or on any other Mississippi public land, for that matter. They're all Bad Birds. But as my wife Jill Easton mentioned in this book's foreword, I'm drawn to difficult turkeys like hummingbirds are drawn to red feeders.

One of my favorite spots on the Homochitto is a place I call the green gate. Behind the gate is a big, diverse chunk of national forest that contains hilly ground, a big creek bottom, open land, brushy clearcuts, big pretty hardwoods, pine plantations, and other land features. It's a great place to find a turkey to play with. But killing one? That's a whole nother proposition.

I got there on Saturday afternoon and lost no time checking

into a little motel that is no longer in business. By 4 p.m. I was in the woods a mile past the green gate, set up on the lip of a long, steep-sided hollow I knew turkeys often roosted in. They didn't do it this day, but I did get into a spirited argument with a hen somewhere off down the hollow, and I noticed the old Lohman was losing that ring that had made it such a killer over the years of our partnership. Like me, it was showing its age.

About an hour before sundown I heard a turkey gobble back toward the gate. I quickly moved that way, wanting to get a better fix on him for tomorrow's hunt. He didn't gobble much, but every once in a while he'd answer that battered old box call, flat notes and all. It was enough for me to keep track of him, and I got close enough to see him when he flew up. After he finished the customary limb-changing and flopping around, he was directly over the access road that started at the green gate, and no more than 150 yards from the gate itself. That put him 155 yards from my truck. Not a good scenario for getting back to the vehicle without disturbing him.

Walking underneath him on the road while it was still light was out of the question, so I waited until dusk turned to full dark. Then I tip-toed under him as quietly as I could, unlocked my truck as stealthily as a cat burglar, and drove back to town wearing a smile wide enough to make my face hurt.

*   *   *

An hour before first light I parked on the blacktop a half-mile short of the gate, then angled through the woods until I hit the access road 500 yards past the gobbler. When dawn cracked I was within 100 yards of him, set up where I could see both the road and the open woods on the downhill side. The uphill side had been lightly logged a decade before, and while not impassable, it wasn't pleasant going either. I was betting the gobbler would pitch down away from the blacktop and walk the access road or through the open woods beside it.

Gobbling time arrived. The cardinals tuned up. Any time now.

Two crows started talking back and forth. Any time now.

A barred owl asked his silly question. *Any. Time. Now.*

But he wasn't talking that day. I tried him with the box. First soft like you're supposed to when your gobbler is still in his tree. Then more aggressive, as desperation kicked in. No response. I didn't see the turkey fly down, but I heard him do it, and I figured any second he'd come slipping along that road. I had my gun up; I was comfortable; I was confident; I was ready.

But when he gobbled, it sounded like he was standing in the middle of the blacktop road. The bird had gone against all logic. He'd flown down the other way and walked under or around the gate. He gobbled again, and sure enough, that's where he was. When he gobbled a third time he was well into the woods across the road, and by the time I gathered my stuff and walked to the gate myself, he was 250 yards into the other woods and going the other way. I followed, but that was the last time I heard him.

That evening he came back. I was again sitting on the lip of that long hollow a mile past the gate, but when he gobbled back toward the gate I went to him again. This time, the aggravating old bird roosted downhill from the road in the open woods, 50 yards farther from the gate but not far enough from the access road that I could get past him while light remained. I waited again, making the mosquitoes happy, and sneaked past the roost again when it got dark.

*   *   *

Surely the gobbler's crossing the paved road had been an aberration. Surely he wouldn't do it again. So my game plan was basically unchanged, except that instead of sitting above the access road I was in the open woods below the road, about 75 yards from where the turkey was sleeping.

He gobbled on the roost this second morning. Again, not a lot, but it gave me hope. He even answered my first run of tree calls on the old box call. But when he flew down, it was again in the direction of the blacktop. He crossed it and I followed, but I did so in a big, looping route that I hoped would let me get ahead of this old road warrior.

I did manage to get ahead of him, but he stopped before he got to me and began a long session of gobbling that lasted more than three hours. This gave me time to get in close and study the situation. He was parked in a big bowl formed by a complicated series of ridges that converged where a wet-weather creek cut a chest-deep channel through the loess soil that makes up that part of the world. It was too open for me to get down in there with him, but he gobbled long enough for me to try calling him in from three of those ridges, using a different call each time. First the Lohman box, then my D.D. Adams slate, then a four-reed cutter mouth call. He answered all of it but he wasn't having any of it, and about ten a.m. he folded his tent.

*   *   *

The gobbler roosted in the same vicinity again that evening, and the next morning I switched tactics. I still parked a half-mile before the green gate, but this time I slipped along the blacktop to the gate, walked 75 yards past it and set up where I could watch both the access road and the open woods. I didn't even reach for a call, except to put a mouth call 'tween cheek and gum for making that sharp *cluck!* that would snap him to attention and seal his fate.

It would have worked, except I set up too far from the stupid gate. He was roosted in the open woods as the day before, and instead of coming to the access road he followed the drain in the open woods and came onto the access road within 10 yards of the gate. Which put him at least 15 yards out of range. I tried to talk him out of it, but it was too little and too late. He gobbled when I yelped and stood there within the radius of the gate's swing for a few minutes, looking for the hen. But then he set his wings, ducked under the green gate and crossed the road for the third day in a row. He beat me to the bowl, and we had pretty much of a replay of the day before.

I was beginning to detect a pattern here.

*   *   *

That afternoon I checked out another of my favored spots. If I'd gotten anything going, I would have abandoned this turkey. But I didn't, so I didn't, if you follow me. This time, though, I went with a different game plan.

I still parked a half-mile down the road, but then I crossed the blacktop, cut cross-country and got to the bowl just as there was enough light to see what I was doing. Also, just as the gobbler I'd been hunting for most of a week started talking. Sure enough, he was over there past the road and past the green gate. So far so good.

I spent the next 20 minutes building a good blind on the toe of one of the ridges where two windthrown beech trees had crossed trunks. By the time I finished, the sound of the gobbling was more muted; he was on the ground.

It was an hour later when I noticed the turkey's infrequent gobbles were getting louder. He was coming, and it was time for me to chime in. They say it's always better to call to a turkey from the place he wants to be, and if this wasn't that place, then where was it?

The sounds coming from the Lohman box were getting pretty flat. I'd tried dressing up the curve of the sounding board with some fine sandpaper the night before, the way Brad Harris had shown me, but it hadn't helped. I'd dressed it so many times over the years I'd worn the curved edge of the sounding board flat, and it no longer made proper contact with the paddle. The result was a flat, one-note yelp, and the cluck sounded more like a duck than a turkey.

I almost left it in my vest. But for some reason this particular gobbler seemed to like that old call, so I got it out, ran a few practice swings of the paddle above the sounding board, then lowered wood to wood and yelped as best I could with the crippled old call.

It sounded awful to my ear, but the approaching gobbler liked it fine, and he gobbled hard from a range of maybe 250 yards. I yelped once more. Again it sounded awful, but the gobbler cut into the back of it with a double gobble that raised the hair on my neck.

I laid the call on the ground and got my gun up. He was there less than a minute later, coming down the opposite ridge into the bowl. At 50 yards I made the slight adjustment that put the bead on his neck. At 40 yards I eased the safety off and shifted the mouth call from my cheek to my tongue.

At 30 yards I clucked. He snapped to attention.

*　*　*

Back at the truck, I went through my normal post-kill ritual. Working off the tailgate, I weighed the gobbler – 17 pounds, 9 ounces, about average for a south Mississippi longbeard. Beards don't interest me nearly as much as spurs, but his was impressive at 11 inches. His spurs were good but not jaw-dropping: one-and-an-eighth and sharp enough to poke a hole in a Coke can.

Then I sat on the tailgate and dug out my father's three-blade Old Timer pocket knife, the knife I carry only when I'm hunting, the only knife I carry when I'm hunting. I held the battered Lohman box in both hands. I held it for a long time. I'd already decided I was retiring the call after this hunt, but there was still something I needed to do.

Turning the call over, I ran my thumb along the double row of notches carved into each edge of the bottom of the walnut box. I hadn't killed every turkey represented by those notches, but I'd been running the call when each of them died. These were the box call's turkeys, not mine.

This final notch I was carving would fill the second row. I carefully finished the job and flipped the tiny wedge of walnut over my shoulder. Then I carefully counted the notches, going up one side of the call and back down the other. I counted them again to make sure. I smiled a little bit.

I sat there on the tailgate for a while, enjoying the morning, thinking about this hunt and past hunts as well. I thought about Brad. I thought about Dad. I thought about Sid and Tommy and Bill and Jimmy and John, all of whom were gone, all of whom had accounted for some of those notches.

My smile was still there, not wide enough to hurt my face but plenty wide enough to tug at my heart. Then I moved Gobbler 80 from the tailgate to the passenger side footwell, so his feathers wouldn't get mussed, and drove away through the sunny Mississippi morning.

Chapter 24

The Phantom

Missouri, 1992. Fellow outdoor writer Michael Pearce and I were checking out turkey hunting opportunities on a smallish state-owned Conservation Area, at the request of Brad Harris, champion competition caller and, at the time, the face and driving force of the now-defunct Lohman Game Calls. We were Lohman's guests for a three-day hunt, and Mike and I had each killed a gobbler the first day. Brad was notoriously stingy with his turkeys, so we figured we were through. But that afternoon Brad pulled us aside.

"You guys interested in doing a little prospecting tomorrow? There's a piece of public land about an hour west of here and I need a scouting report on it. I'll furnish gas and a vehicle."

Asking Mike Pearce or me if we want to go turkey hunting is like asking a piranha if he wants red meat. We were on it like white on rice, and next morning we were out the door and on the road before the rest of the camp even woke up.

It was a good-looking place – 1600 acres and a bit, mostly good hardwood timber with a few open areas, hilly but not too steep or rough. Good turkey country, and no other cars in the small parking lot. Dawn was just breaking as we took the trail out of the parking lot, and we hadn't gone far when turkeys started gobbling everywhere. Up the hill in front of us. Behind us, along the road we'd driven to get to the parking lot. Across the creek bottom east of the parking lot. Along a long narrow field we'd seen as we drove into the place.

Nothing was very close, but it's hard to not be optimistic when you're listening to turkeys at every point of the compass. Things were definitely looking up. We decided to stay on the trail and keep climbing. There were at least two gobblers in that direction, and higher is almost always better than lower when you're hunting unfamiliar territory.

By the time we got to the top, though, everything had gone quiet up there. There was a small stand of good-sized planted pines on flat ground at the head of a big hollow, maybe an acre's worth. They stood out from the surrounding hardwoods, and the little plantation looked like a prime listening spot. Standing beside it, Mike ran a series of yelps on his box call (a Lohman, naturally) and a turkey gobbled in the hollow below us, back in the general direction of the truck. We gained a couple hundred yards on him, but after gobbling three more times he ran out of things to say.

But our set-up was good and the woods were pretty. It was still early, not yet 7 a.m., and in the absence of any further gobbling we elected to sit tight for a while rather than prowl around and risk boogering non-gobbling turkeys. At 8:30 we still hadn't heard anything, but that might have been because we'd both slept through most of the intervening 90 minutes. Whatever the reason, we decided sitting in one place wasn't going to give us much to report to Brad, so we climbed back to the top of the hollow and moved slowly through the spring greenery, stopping every little while to call and listen.

At the third or fourth stop, a gobbler answered Mike's trusty box. Again, down in the hollow – probably the same one we'd set up on earlier. We moved closer and set up. He gobbled a couple more times and shut up again. We moved a little closer, sat down on a brushy knob that sort of stuck out into the hollow and parked ourselves again to wait him out. Nothing happened. A half-hour later I clucked and purred as soft as I could on a true slate, and the resulting gobble nearly blew my hat off.

He was right under the lip of the knob we were on, and it became immediately apparent we'd sat down wrong. We had good long-range visibility in all directions, but in close we were blind. The brush on the knob and the steepness of its slope hid everything from 15 to 75 yards, and the gobbler was in that blind zone. He gobbled again on his own, and he was closer. Then I could hear him drumming. He was so close I could hear the leaves rustle as he dragged his wings through them, and even then, more than 20 years ago, my battered old duck hunter's ears had trouble picking up that frequency. He was *close*. Our guns were up. Our safeties were off. If we saw him, he'd be right on top of us.

We never saw him. After a while the drumming and leaf-raking stopped. I clucked and purred again. He gobbled, but from a distance. He'd left us and there was no getting him back. We pilfered around the rim of that hollow until the one o'clock bell. We heard him a few more times down in there, sometimes answering us and sometimes gobbling for his own private reasons, but nothing we did could convince him to come up for another visit.

* * *

The next morning we were back, and this time we arrived early enough to make it to the top before gobbling time. The two turkeys we'd heard up there yesterday were still home, and when they started gobbling they were in the planted pines, less than 200 yards from us. We cut the distance to 150 and sat down shoulder to shoulder.

These were strange turkeys. They roosted less than 50 feet apart, but when they flew down, they flew in opposite directions. One sailed on a long slant through the open hardwoods to the east, crossing onto private land before touching down. We didn't see the other one fly down, but apparently he just leaned forward and fell off his limb. Both gobbled some after they flew down, but they made no move to get back together. After a little while, the private land gobbler hushed. Henned up, probably.

The other one, though, seemed interested in our calling. He fell into one of those aggravating back-and-forth patterns, coming toward us for a while and then retreating to the pines where he'd spent the night. At his closest he was probably inside 50 yards, but he stayed just far enough down the slope at the head of the hollow to remain hidden. After making three or four laps, he drifted off into the hollow like he'd done yesterday. We gave him enough time to put distance between us and then took rounders, going back along the hollow on the high ground for a quarter-mile and then dropping into the hollow with him.

He helped us by gobbling every once in a while, and when we were down on his level and 250 yards away we set up again. He came, he gobbled, he drummed, he left. We moved on him and called some more. He came, he gobbled, he drummed. He left.

How that turkey managed to do this is still a mystery, but we fooled with him until 10:30, moved on him six times, called him into gun range three times, and never once did we lay an eyeball on him. When we finally lost contact, Mike said: "Let's get out of here. This turkey is a phantom, and phantoms are bulletproof."

* * *

Mike had to leave for home that day, and the Lohman turkey camp was officially ending. But I had an extra day before I had to be anywhere, so I decided to stick around for one more try at The Phantom.

I was waiting near the planted pines when daylight arrived that final morning, and The Phantom didn't disappoint. He and his bunkmate were roosted in the pines, and true to pattern, they went opposite directions when they flew down.

But I was one step ahead this time. Or so I thought. At the first gobble, I backed off from the pines and dropped into the hollow, then crept back up the hollow until I had the pines in sight. I sat down against a comfortable tree and waited for The Phantom to walk into my lap.

Three hours later I was still waiting. He flew down at the normal time, did his usual gobbling routine, but this morning he never acknowledged my calling. When he finally came into the hollow he was on the other slope and 40 yards out of range, but at least I got my first look at him as he went by.

I let him get well out of sight and then dropped all the way to the bottom of the hollow and hustled along it, trying to get ahead of him. After a while I could see some sort of opening ahead. It turned out to be a long, narrow, grassy opening that followed the lowest part of the hollow. It ran for a couple hundred yards, varying in width from 50 feet to 50 yards. It looked like a place turkeys would like, so I moved partway down the opening, found a spot on the east side with good visibility that would stay shaded until past midday, and tucked myself in. I didn't know if I was ahead of The Phantom or behind him, but I figured it didn't make any difference. Like Mike said, phantoms are bulletproof.

Calling intermittently, I sat there as the morning morphed into midday. Over that few hours, a turkey gobbled three times far down the hollow, at the limit of hearing. I ignored him.

It was twelve noon exactly when I made another call. I was as surprised as anybody when a hen immediately cut me off. I gave it right back to her and she came out of the woods 100 yards down the hollow, yelping and cutting nonstop. I gave it right back to her, and when she had closed the distance by half I saw The Phantom step out of the woods behind her, in full strut. I stopped calling, but the hen didn't. She marched right to me, and I tried to become my tree.

At 30 feet she put on the foot brakes but not the beak brakes. She stood there in the gently waving grass and berated me for three or four minutes before running out of steam, and then she just wandered off. Meanwhile, the gobbler hadn't moved an inch toward me. But he hadn't left either, so that gave me hope.

Thirty minutes later it was 12:35, and he still hadn't moved. Five more minutes. No movement. Time was running out fast. At 12:45 I decided desperate measures were called for. The grass in the long opening was only a foot high, but the dry creek drain in the hollow was a foot deeper than the dirt surrounding it. If I could make it to that drain, maybe I could low-crawl close enough for a kill.

Long odds, but it seemed to be my only play. I shrugged off my vest and carefully rolled off my tree into the open place, feeling more exposed than a Sports Illustrated swimsuit model. Pushing the old 870 ahead of me, I wiggled across the 15 feet of sparse grass separating me from the run of the creek. I couldn't tell whether I'd gotten away with it or not, but I wasn't about to raise my head for a look-see.

Before starting on this fool's errand, I'd picked out a dead snag for a landmark. When I reached it, I'd be within 30 to 35 yards of the gobbler. Or at least within that distance of where he'd been when I started. When I reached the snag I glanced at my watch. 12:53. Show time.

Very carefully, I crawled my upper body part of the way out of the drain and raised my head as slow as the sunrise. And there he was, sideways to me, still strutting, still in that same spot. I didn't want to shoot him in strut, so I put my gun on him, worked up enough spit to operate the mouth call, and clucked to get him to raise his head.

Instead, he gobbled, and it surprised me so much I didn't shoot. I clucked again, sharper this time, and he gobbled again.

Okay, buddy, have it your way. I adjusted my aim, moving the bead from just above his topknot to just ahead of his beak, and clucked again. He gobbled, moving his head into the sweet spot.

Jill J Easton

Phantoms aren't bulletproof.

Mike was wrong. Phantoms aren't bulletproof. I stood up, walked over to him, and looked at my watch just as 12:59 went away and 1:00 took its place.

Chapter 25

The Jinx of Fire Tower Ridge

We were going in on second-hand information. That can be risky, but I trusted my source. Anyway, the report sounded so good we simply had to check it out. Our friend had left a voicemail message the previous afternoon:

"Hey, I killed a good one this morning about a mile in on the ridge that runs west from the fire tower and I heard seven more birds gobbling in there. I'm leaving for Kansas in a few minutes but I wanted to let you know about 'em. Merry Christmas."

Friends like that are good to have. I called him back and picked his brain while he was driving. Next morning I dropped Jill off at the tower (more accurately, I dropped her where it used to be; the tower itself has been gone for 25 years, but everybody still calls the place "the fire tower".) Then I drove around on a looping series of Forest Service roads to the west end of the ridge and parked on the edge of a hay field that belonged to a neighbor. The field wrapped around the western toe of the ridge, and crossing it was the only way to get to that toe.

When I called my neighbor the night before to get permission, he told me he'd been seeing two gobblers in the pasture almost every morning through the winter and early spring, and he didn't think anybody had hunted them. Good news. I was running a few minutes late, and sure enough, I could hear two turkeys gobbling up near the top of the ridge as I crossed the pasture.

I had an easy time setting up on them, because I decided not to climb the ridge. If the turkeys had been using the field for months, why not just wait for them to come there? I crossed the fence, found a good tree about 50 yards into the woods, and made myself comfortable.

Good thing I decided to stay downhill, because I hadn't been in my hide for more than five minutes when I heard a commotion of limbs and wings, and the gobblers came sailing down the side of the ridge like a couple of ungainly, overweight buzzards. One of them passed 75 yards to my left and sailed 60 yards into the field, but the other one pulled up short and touched down in the woods, slightly above my level and 80 yards off the gun.

My hunt should have been over in 30 minutes. The gobbler politely and eagerly answered my calls, went immediately into strut, and started working his way toward me, stopping to strut every few steps, gobbling occasionally. He was coming slowly, but he was coming, so I didn't slow him down any more by calling. It took him 25 minutes to cover 50 yards, and then he stepped into a little open spot at 30 yards and struck a pose in a patch of golden early morning sunshine. He was drumming hard, puffed up as round as a blowfish, completely mesmerized by his own gorgeous self.

It was the entire package, the experience we always hope for but so seldom get. I already had my gun on him. All I had to do was wait until he raised his head, then shoot him.

At the time, I was nearly 30 years into hunting turkeys. You'd think I'd have been up to the simple task of shooting a suicidal gobbler that was standing still and erect at the optimum distance from the barrel. But I managed to screw it up anyway.

When he raised his head, I pulled the trigger – and missed him clean. I know exactly what I did wrong; I've done it more than a dozen times. I was as wrapped up in the gobbler's performance as the gobbler was himself. He was so handsome as he came in, and when he stopped in that spotlight it was one of the most beautiful things I've ever seen in the woods. And, wanting an unobstructed view, I didn't have my stupid head down on my stupid gun. When I pulled the stupid trigger, the stupid pattern passed two stupid feet over the stupid gobbler's stupid head.

I missed him so bad he didn't even know he'd been shot at. This I know because instead of running, he gobbled. He heard the report of the gun, of course, and it startled him – which is exactly why he shock-gobbled. I suppose I could have killed him if I'd shot at him again, but I was so flabbergasted I just sat there and watched him for the two or three seconds it took him to compose himself and decide to get out of there. By the time I realized I still had a loaded gun to my shoulder, he was leaving – not running but almost – with that herky-jerky head motion turkeys have when they're nervous but trying to be cool about it.

I didn't feel comfortable with the shot so I held off, and then he was gone. About 10 minutes later I heard Jill shoot. She doesn't miss very often. For some odd reason, though, the sound of her gun reminded me of the second gobbler, the one that had sailed past me and landed in the pasture. I'd forgotten all about him.

I shifted around my tree and used binoculars to scan what I could see of the field. Nothing visible. Getting to my feet, I used tree trunks as much as possible as I advanced one slow step at a time toward the fence, stopping every few steps to glass the field again. I was still 20 yards from the fence when I spotted him way out there, strutting along behind three oblivious hens.

They were in bright sunlight and I was in heavy shade with a little brush to break my outline, so I leaned against a convenient tree and watched. The hens were feeding, obviously without a destination in mind, and they wandered aimlessly around in loops and circles. Hens and gobbler alike ignored the two or three series of calls I made, and it was quickly becoming obvious I wasn't going to get anywhere with this strategy.

But it's my policy to avoid spooking turkeys unnecessarily, and the only way I could get to my truck was by crossing that pasture. I decided to wait a while and see if they might leave the field on their own. The morning was still young, so I eased ten yards closer to the fence, found a comfortable tree and settled in.

I guess the tree was a little *too* comfortable. When I woke up I was disoriented and for a minute didn't know where I was. A glance at my watch told me I'd been out for more than two hours. I was getting myself together and preparing to stand up when it came clear exactly what had awakened me. A roaring gobble erupted from directly in front of me, maybe 20 yards into the field. I froze in place and leaned very slowly left to see around the tree blocking my view, and there he was, the second gobbler of the morning I'd seen strutting at close range in full sunlight.

I don't think he saw me when I peered around the tree. But I made a mistake when I jerked my head back out of sight too fast. I was now hidden again, but he'd caught a movement and it made him suspicious. He didn't gobble any more, but I saw him walk to my left when he came out from behind the tree, and he was no longer strutting. He was single-footing now, angling away from me, but moving slow and still well within gun range. I brought the stupid gun up slow and smooth and effortlessly executed my second stupid miss of the stupid morning. I have no idea what I did wrong that time.

At least this one had the courtesy to fly after the shot, and he did it straight over the top of my truck, parked at the pasture gate on the county road. Well, no turkey to keep me from crossing the pasture now. I rolled under the bottom wire of the fence, stood up and thereby committed my third faux pas of the hunt. When I got to my feet I looked down the fence line just in time to see another gobbler run out of the field and into the woods 150 yards away.

For somebody whose policy is to avoid spooking turkeys

unnecessarily, I was sure spooking a lot of turkeys this morning. I'd made enough screw-ups for one day and it was time to go ooh and aah over Jill's turkey anyway, so I left. Sure enough, she hadn't missed, and the gobbler was impressive, with sharp spurs and a good beard. As she told me the story, I tried my best to be happy for her. I think I was convincing.

*   *   *

I had a dentist appointment early the next morning – yes, poor planning on my part during turkey season – so I didn't get to the woods until after ten. I wasn't planning to hunt the field or Fire Tower Ridge that day, but I drove by there on the way to hunt elsewhere. There were three gobblers in the field, and they snapped to attention and watched me drive by.

I located a workable gobbler ten miles away from Fire Tower Ridge just before noon, but he had a couple of jakes with him and one of them got too far in front of the big boy. He came gawking and yawking straight to me, and when he was less than 10 feet away he picked me out and spooked. The longbeard was still ten yards out of shotgun range, but he spooked too. He didn't know what he was spooking from, but he didn't like the situation so he left.

I liked the way he'd come to the call, though, so I went back to try him again the next morning. About 7 a.m. he came in again, this time without any company, and it worked out badly for him.

*   *   *

After two days' rest, I hoped the field birds would be calmed back down, but none of them gobbled near the pasture that next morning. There were three gobbling from the top of Fire Tower Ridge, though, and by the time I flanked them and climbed to their level, they were on the ground and moving. But not downhill toward the pasture. They stayed on top and went east, and I had no choice but to tag along behind.

I tried to drop off the side of the ridge and get ahead of them, but it was rough going and I couldn't travel fast enough. I lost them and couldn't get anything else going that day.

*　　*　　*

I went in earlier the next morning and crossed the pasture in the dark. Once across the fence, I climbed three-quarters of the way to the top and listened from there, in case the turkeys roosted closer to the pasture this time. They were on top again, and this time I was close enough I got there well before they flew down. I circled and got on the ridgetop past the turkeys, setting up along the route they'd taken the day before.

But I guessed wrong again. It was getting monotonous. They headed downhill toward the pasture, and as soon as they were on the downslope I hurried to the end of Fire Tower Ridge and cut hard at them. All three gobbled, 250 yards downhill. A minute later I did it again, and all three gobbled again. The difference was, this time two of the gobblers were farther downhill, but the third one seemed to be coming back to me.

He circled around me as he climbed, and I shifted to follow him as he did. By the time he closed he was coming at me from straight uphill, disproving the old belief that a turkey won't come downhill to a call. I saw him at about 80 yards, got my gun up when he went behind a tree at 70. When he went behind another tree at 45 yards I adjusted my aim and waited. He gave me the shot I wanted at between 35 and 40 yards. I made sure I was down on the gun and pulled the trigger. And pulled. And pulled some more.

By the time I realized I'd forgotten to take the gun off safety, the gobbler had stood still long enough to get nervous. He wasn't seeing the hen. He was just starting to turn when I punched the safety button hard, and it sounded as loud as a cue ball breaking a tight rack.

He was in motion immediately, running back up the mountain but straight away, and I shot him in the back of the head – I thought.

He flew, and I watched in disbelief. That's when I saw the inch-thick sapling topple over a half-dozen feet in front of my gun barrel.

*   *   *

I hunted that ridge and the pasture four more days after that, and I never did kill a turkey there. One day they didn't gobble. Another day a coyote messed up the hunt. Another day another hunter came in from the other side and I backed off. I forget what went wrong the fourth day, but it was something. I was well and truly jinxed at that place, and I decided to quit going there before the jinx infected my luck elsewhere. I already have enough trouble killing turkeys without laboring under a cloud of juju.

That was more than 15 years ago. I haven't hunted Fire Tower Ridge, or the pasture, in those intervening years. Maybe I'll try it this spring.

Or maybe not.

Chapter 26

George

Opening Day, 2022. Arkansas. We'd gotten home from a week-long Texas expedition the day before, so I was going in blind. I'd looked the place over one morning three weeks earlier and had found a little sign, but nothing to get all worked up about.

But this was a sleeper location: at only 800 acres not big enough to attract much attention in an area with abundant public hunting land. But it had good hardwood timber, five food plots, steep ridges and hollows with a good stretch of flat land in the middle, and it had water on three sides. It also had a hiking trail network that provided quick and easy access. Icing on the cake, it was well camouflaged from turkey hunters because to reach it you had to drive through an unincorporated rich-retirees subdivision. I'd been hunting the place for maybe ten years and only once encountered another hunter. I figured it would be a good Opening Day choice because most of the pressure would be concentrated on the large national forest less than 20 miles away.

Sure enough, when I drove through the subdivision well before dawn, I found the small parking area empty. Two hiking trails led out of the lot. Both led to good woods. I arbitrarily chose the left trail. In case somebody else came in behind me, I left a note taped to the tailgate of my truck: *"I went west."*

I didn't go far, though. Sometimes turkeys roosted near the back yards of the houses closest to the hunting area. They didn't this morning, but I was still glad I didn't go in very far. I was leaning against a black cherry at the edge of a tennis-court sized grassy opening when he gobbled across the cleared space and another 80 yards or so into the open woods beyond. I had a good lock on his direction. There were two big, overmature shortleaf pines that way. I figured him to be in one of them.

He was really too close and there was too much light for me to do what I did, but if I was going to have a chance at this gobbler I badly needed to cross that grassy opening. He gobbled again, and I figured out which of the pines he was in. He gobbled again and I couldn't see him. Daylight was growing fast; time to roll the dice. Hoping he was on the other side of the trunk, I scooted across the opening going straight at the pine tree to minimize my angle of exposure. I barely made it into the woods when he gobbled again, and this time he was on the ground.

I called to the gobbler before moving, and he answered me immediately. He was maybe 200 yards from me, due south, not far from the tree he'd slept in. That told me I hadn't spooked him. If I had, he'd have stayed in the tree or sailed a long way away when he flew down.

One of the hiking trails in this piece of ground ran under the two big pines, and it sounded like the gobbler was on or very near that trail. It joined a larger trail about 150 yards east of me, and I headed that way, figuring it would be a good place to set up.

I figured right, but I was too slow. I was halfway to the trail junction when he gobbled again, and that's where he already was – at the trail junction. I was too close to risk the noise of setting up, so I just stepped behind the nearest big tree and got my gun up, bracing against the tree and standing erect. I yelped softly on the diaphragm call that stays tucked in my cheek when I'm hunting, and the turkey cut me off.

Seconds later he stepped into the big trail and stood there in the open, looking my way. I had my finger on the trigger and the safety was off. Only one thing kept my finger from tightening. He was 20 yards out of range.

He stood there for a good three minutes and didn't move anything. Neither me. I was sending him a furious barrage of telepathic thoughts, though: *Come on, you know you want it. Get on down here. All you need to do is come just a little bit this way. Come on. Come on…*

And miracle of miracles, he did. Or rather, he started doing it. He was single-footing, the way a deer will do when it's in high alert but not yet spooked. Step. Pause. Look. Step. Pause. Look. Step. Pause. Look.

At about the dozenth step-pause-look sequence, I was getting confident. This gobbler was going to single-foot right into gun range and I was going to kill an opening-day gobbler in my home state, something I hadn't done in several years. I was already thinking about how easy this carry back to the truck was going to be.

He did it twice more. Step. Pause. Look. Step. Pause. Look. I judged the range at 55 yards. With TSS, my gun delivers a lethal pattern at that range, but my self-imposed limit is 50, just in case I misjudge the distance a little. Like most other experienced turkey hunters, I prefer 25- to 35-yard shots, but, full disclosure, I'm not that hard-headed about it.

That was when things went sideways. Or at least, the gobbler did. For no reason that I could discern (other than the fact that he was an adult gobbler and therefore one of the least predictable creatures on the planet,) he stood there at 55 yards until I could feel my gun barrel getting noticeably heavier. Then, with no panic or concern in his demeanor, he executed a military right face and walked into the woods on the other side of the trail. He circled around me, stopping every few steps, but my goose was cooked and I knew it. When he was out of sight he started gobbling again, but even though I repositioned on him three or four times over the next two hours while I tried to flank him and keep up, it was futile. I finally lost him – or he lost me, however you want to look at it – about ten o'clock and didn't have any more action that day.

*   *   *

Jill hadn't found any action at her spot that day, so we tried a double-team effort the next morning. The turkey was nowhere to be found, although we stayed in there moving and calling, using the trail network to move swiftly and silently, until nearly 3 p.m. We covered the entire 800 acres and never heard a turkey noise or saw a turkey.

Two days later we went back, and almost killed him. He was roosted in another big pine above one of the trails, more than half a mile from where I'd found him the first day. We bumped two hens as we went to him, but it was a good thing – they flew out over the lake and all the way across, removing themselves from the equation. The racket did shut the gobbler up for a few minutes, but he got his motor running again and we were able to set up within 125 yards of him. He was on one side of a shallow bowl, we were on the other at about his level. We saw him leave the tree, sailing in our general direction but landing 60 yards away and out of sight under a fold of ground near the uphill end of the bowl. He gobbled a few times as he approached, and then we both heard him drumming just over the last part of the rise.

Let me tell you about my wife and me and drumming turkeys: Jill is almost completely deaf in her left ear, and due to four decades of duck hunting (half of it as a guide) my poor old eardrums have just about surrendered. When either of us can hear a turkey drumming, the time has long passed when we should have had the gun mounted and the safety showing red.

Jill shifted her gun just a little to aim at the sound. That's exactly what she should have done, but the unfortunate thing is, standing right behind her when she did it was a jake that had been coming to the gobbler along the hiking trail. He caught the movement and started clucking and walking away. It didn't spook the longbeard but it changed his mind, and though he kept gobbling he started moving away. He crossed the bowl and we saw him as he came up the other side. He walked under his roost tree and on to the west, and we followed him to a big pine ridge where he set up shop. We were able to get above him and got him coming again, but something happened when he was still 90 to 100 yards out. He abruptly stopped gobbling, we heard wingbeats, then nothing. A coyote or bobcat rushed him, maybe. Whatever, it ended the encounter, and when a heavy thunderstorm started 30 minutes later it ended the hunt.

The turkey now qualified as a Bad Bird, and Bad Birds need names. I named this one George. There's a reason, but I can't explain it to you because it would give away the location of the place. I'd probably like you if I met you – most turkey hunters are decent people, I've found. But I definitely do NOT want to meet you on that 800 acres.

We hunted George again the next morning, but this time separately. Jill went back to the section of trail where we worked him, and I went back to the area where I'd found him the first day. Neither of us heard anything, but when we met at the truck in late morning, we could barely hear one gobbling down a section of trail neither of us had covered that morning. George evidently had itchy feet. We got on him quickly and without any trouble, since he was close to a long section of trail that ran the spine of a steep ridge. But he was in one of the food plots and we couldn't get close enough to the edge to shoot into the open area, and he wouldn't come into the woods with us. He strutted around in the food plot, we could see him plainly, but he wasn't buying what we were selling. Eventually he left, going the other way, and we never made contact again.

*   *   *

Four days passed before we went back. George was still there, but now there were three other turkeys gobbling around the property. We thought about trying one of the new birds, but George was closest, and anyway we were mad at him. He wasn't far from where I'd worked him the first day, and we made our set close enough that we heard him fly down. After a spell of calling and gobbling and no movement on George's part, we were in the process of relocating when we nearly ran face to face with a gobbler coming toward George from one of the food plots. He gobbled just in time to alert us of his presence, and, caught in the open, we fell on our bellies just before he popped into view at 70 yards. We watched him go by, circled and got between him and George, but it didn't work out. George left the high ground for the first time since we'd hunted him. He dropped off the flat and went down to the water, and the other gobbler either went with him or disappeared. Either way, George quit gobbling.

Jill elected to follow George down by the lake, but it was wasted effort. I went to where we'd heard two of the new gobblers and found one of them. He played hard to get as well. I worked him for two hours and saw him twice, once at 90 yards as he was coming and at 125 or so as he was leaving. This 800 acres was beginning to get under my skin.

*   *   *

But the next day George died. It happened this way: Once again he was the only turkey we could hear gobbling, and once again he was close to one of the hiking trails. We got to him fast and quiet, made a good set and I tree called to him. He cut me off and we heard him fly down. He set about making his customary racket on the ground, and it sounded like he was walking a back-and-forth route of about 100 to 150 yards, coming toward us until he got 75 or so yards away, then going back the other way until we thought we'd lost him. Then he'd turn around and march back, filling us with false hope.

He did this three or four times. We formulated a plan. When George got almost to his far turnaround spot, I got up and moved forward 75 yards, then set up at about his near turnaround point. Jill stayed at our original set-up spot and continued to call. I'd wanted to do it the other way around, but Jill said no, I'd found the turkey, I should be the one to kill him. We didn't have time to argue.

I was almost to my new spot and George had just gobbled at the far end of his track when the woods shook with what I swear was the loudest shotgun report I've ever heard. I got my wits back just as Jill walked up to me. We could hear two voices down the trail, laughing, talking excitedly. The words weren't understandable at that distance, but the emotion was: ebullience.

I looked at Jill. Jill looked at me. "You want to go down there and see what he looks like?" I asked.

"What for?" she said.

Chapter 27

The Bad-Asses
of Bennington County

For decades now, whenever I find fresh turkey sign, I call from that spot before going any farther. It's a rule of thumb that's served me well. So when Jill spotted the fresh gobbler turd in the trail not 50 yards from where we'd parked, I ran through a calling routine – box, true slate, glass pot-and-peg, wingbone, trumpet, diaphragm, pausing a minute or so between calls. It took five minutes or so. Nothing answered.

Jill wasn't impressed. She poked at the dropping with her boot. "'Taste that, world-class turkey caller. We need to know what they're eating."

My wife the humorist.

We were in Vermont, hunting public land. It was mid-afternoon, hot, windy, the last week of the season. We'd never laid eyes on the place before we walked into it. It was a stacked-deck scenario for sure, but you have to accept stacked decks when you're turkey hunters with (a) limited finances and (b) a driving desire to hunt new places.

So we hiked further in, 50 yards from the truck being a little too close to start a hunt, and hadn't gone another hundred yards before we bumped the gobbler that had probably left the sign. The trail dropped over the edge of a steep incline, and he thundered into the air just off the trail as we reached the downhill plunge. Again my wife was not impressed, and again she gave me the stink-eye.

Was he coming up the hill to the calls? Had he been there all along, listening but ignoring? Who knew, so why was my wife blaming me for it? It was another of turkey hunting's unanswerable questions, but it did make us decide we needed to sit down for a while and hunt with our ears instead of our feet. Since the drop-off overlooked a big hollow that stretched each way farther than we could see, this was as good a spot as any.

Fifteen minutes later, Jill ran a yelp-cut sequence on an old Black Mystic box call she's been carrying for years. From the south, far down the hollow, a gobbler answered. Not the one we'd bumped; he flew in the opposite direction. But then he gobbled, too, and the first gobbler answered him. Hmmm. Less than 30 minutes into our hunt, and we – she, as Jill was quick to point out – had two turkeys gobbling. Maybe this deck wasn't so stacked after all.

But it was, of course, or this wouldn't be a Bad Birds story.

Both gobblers were on the opposite side of the hollow, each of them 400 to 500 yards away. We needed to cross. It wasn't a deep hollow, but the pitch on both sides was steep. Jill and I are no longer as spry as teenagers, and it took us a while. Meanwhile, the gobblers had struck up a conversation. By the time we climbed to their level on the opposite hillside, we were listening to a spirited gobbling match, and both participants were getting closer.

We made our stand just off the top of the next hillside, with the turkeys slightly below our level and closing steadily. We had them pegged to follow the contour of a narrow bench that passed 30 yards below our set, and it seemed for a while we'd guessed right. But then they did what turkeys often do. Instead of meeting just below us within perfect shotgun range, they shared some sort of turkey telepathy and left the bench, walked straight uphill and got together on top, within shotgun range but out of sight beyond the curve of the slope.

It happened fast, and by the time we realized what was happening it was too late to adjust to it. We scooted around our trees to face uphill but still couldn't see over the lip, not even when we stood up. And we missed seeing a heck of a gobbler fight. Purring, wing-popping, the whole catastrophe. Maybe we could have sneaked straight uphill and killed one or both while they were thus occupied, but on public land sneaking turkeys is a good way to get shot. And anyway, it seemed then, and still seems now, sort of like cheating.

So we stood there helplessly, within killing distance of two fighting turkeys, and never saw a feather. The fight didn't last long – they rarely do, in my experience – and when it was over and all was quiet on top, I motioned to Jill to remain standing but get behind her tree with her gun up. I retreated 30 yards downhill and put together a short but vehement string of yelps and cuts, using both diaphragm and box. Surely the winner of the fight would come take a look. *Surely* he would.

Five minutes later I did it again. One turkey gobbled – I assume it was the winner – but he was 150 yards away. When he gobbled on his own two minutes later, he was farther, and that's the last turkey sound we heard that day.

*   *   *

The next morning we were back across that hollow, standing where the fight took place. Three turkeys gobbled. Two were on our side of the hollow, and the third sounded like he was roosted over the truck. The two gobblers on our side were 300 to 400 yards apart and we were between them. It was a good tactical position, but it hadn't helped us the day before. The winner of yesterday's fight had gone west, so that's the one we chose. Our logic was, well, logical: we figured he was the one most likely to respond to our calling, since he'd licked the other bird.

221

We closed the distance as much as we felt we could get away with and set up on the flat ground above the hollow, about 125 yards from the turkey. Both gobblers were still yelling at each other, but when our bird flew down and gobbled from the ground, the turkey behind us quit gobbling.

Jill was 25 yards ahead of me and facing the dominant gobbler at 12 o'clock. I set up facing 3 o'clock with her and the gobbler off my left shoulder, so I could guard our back door in case the now-quiet gobbler came sneaking in. I thought I was being clever, you see.

Imagine my surprise when the now-quiet gobbler (or maybe it was the one from back at the truck) cut loose with a ferocious double gobble directly behind me. I don't know exactly how close he was, but I'm guessing feet, not yards. Close enough, at any rate, for me to hear that breathy rattle at the bottom of the gobble.

I'd have had a better chance with him if he'd been a thousand yards away. As it was, all I could do was sit there and hope against all hope he'd walk somewhere that would let me see him. And…he… didn't. When he gobbled the second time he was considerably farther away and still straight behind me, going down into the hollow. The third time, he was farther yet.

I didn't know until later that Jill already had the dominant bird in sight for quite a while. He'd been slowly coming toward her, strutting but not gobbling, and she had her gun on him at 60 yards when the bird behind me gobbled the first time. The strutting gobbler went sideways and so did the hunt. Instead of continuing along the high ground path that would have brought him into range, he skirted Jill and went downhill into the hollow and was quickly out of sight, presumably getting with the other gobbler and either leading him or maybe chasing him down into the hollow.

Either way, our hunt – for those two birds at least – was over for the day. We heard one of them gobble 30 minutes later, far down the hollow, and then nothing. Nothing for the rest of the day, in fact.

*   *   *

The third day (second morning) in Vermont, we again listened from the same spot. The two gobblers had evidently kissed and made up, because this morning they were roosted together but farther down the hollow, barely within hearing. We had to hustle to get close to them before they flew down, and when they did we couldn't do a thing with them. They gobbled at us a lot but kept moving away. We circled below them and tried to get ahead two or three times, but each time they were moving too fast for us to pull it off. When they crossed into posted property at ten a.m., we were more than two miles from where we'd started. We hunted our way back to the truck, but when the midday bell rang we'd found no more action.

*   *   *

We debated trying a new place the third morning, but it's hard to leave gobbling turkeys in favor of the unknown, especially when time is running short. We had this day to hunt plus two or three hours the next morning, and then we had to leave for Pennsylvania. Better the devil you know…

We did make a change, though. Because the gobblers had moved so far the day before, we got there early enough to walk almost a mile that way before gobbling time. Sure enough, the gobblers were still together and still a couple hundred yards into the private land. We set up 50 yards from the line and listened to them gobble in tandem for almost an hour past normal fly-down time, and when they finally had their feet on the ground we went to work on them.

And wonder of wonders, they began to come. We heard them get into another fight – somebody was evidently a slow learner – but again it only lasted a few seconds. The woods were open, with a closed canopy and very little groundline vegetation, and about ten minutes after the fight we picked up movement. They were still nearly a hundred yards on their side of the property boundary. The dominant bird was strutting but wouldn't let his subordinate do anything except tag along and gobble. Every time Number Two tried to fuzz up, the big boy slicked down and made a run at him. The gobblers zig-zagged through the woods toward us, slowly closing the gap until they were just short of the line.

And there they stopped. Fifty-five yards short of Jill's raised gun barrel, less than ten yards from being legal, they stopped. For what reason I do not know; turkeys can't read (they can't, right?) and there was nothing to mark the line except posted signs and Forest Service red paint. But despite turkey illiteracy, despite a complete absence of physical obstacles, they…stopped. *Stopped*, dammit!

I don't know how long they stood there, looking our way, motionless as yard gnomes. All I know for sure is, it was a long time. My nose started itching. Then my back. Then a root grew under my butt. Then a bluebottle fly decided my right ear was interesting. Then my nose itch morphed into an irrepressible need to sneeze.

I held it as long as I could; I held it until tears were running down my cheeks; I held it until I was afraid to breathe for fear it would get away from me. When it broke through despite my best efforts, it was not the bell-ringer I so needed it to be. More like the snort of a very small pig. But it broke the stalemate. The gobblers quit impersonating yard art, set their wings in unison, reversed direction and marched back into the safety of the private land. I waited until they were out of sight before throwing my hat to the ground.

*   *   *

The final morning, Jill decided to stay close to the truck and try for the gobbler that had been roosting there. We'd heard him all

This is how I imagined the more dominant Bad-Ass would look all the while we were hunting him. I was disappointed when he just looked like a turkey.

three mornings we'd hunted, and never more than a quarter-mile from where we always parked. Hardhead that I am, I went back to the Bad-ass and his buddy.

They were still on the private land, but this time a lot closer to the property line. We'd been calling pretty conservatively to these two turkeys, but this morning I pulled all the stops. I tree yelped at them when they started gobbling, waited until they flew down and then did my best impersonation of a double fly-down cackle, row-row-row-your-boat style, with a diaphragm and a slate. Then I yelped a good bit with a box and a diaphragm, slowly building the excitement level until I even got myself a little worked up.

While I was making all this racket the gobblers were going

crazy, and when I came to a logical stopping point in a long string of box call cutting and cackling mixed with excited diaphragm hen yelps, I abruptly cut it off. Both turkeys gobbled six or seven more times in rapid succession, but I stayed quiet. And then here they came, not at a sprint but almost.

Evidently all my pedal-to-the-metal calling broke something in their dominance hierarchy, because this time I detected no hint of a boss/lackey relationship in the footrace coming at me. One gobbler would be ahead for a few seconds, then the other would push to the front. They covered 150 yards in less than a minute, and when the first turkey broke the 40-yard mark I squawked on the diaphragm. They stopped, and I killed the closest one.

I have no idea which turkey it was, boss or subordinate, but it didn't matter. They were both Bad-asses.

Icing on the cake, I was halfway back to the truck when I heard Jill shoot. She was sitting on the tailgate when I got there, with a grin a foot wide and a turkey bigger than mine.

Chapter 28

The Magic Roost

Spoiler alert: this is not a Bad Birds tale. Rather, it's a tale of…well, decide for yourself:

I was west of San Angelo, Texas, early April, 2004. We were hunting at Adobe Lodge, which back then was a top-notch deer and turkey destination place. It probably still is, but I can't say for sure because as of this writing (August 2023) it's been a decade since I've been there and camp owner and head honcho Skipper Duncan has gone on to his reward.

Anyway…

This was one of those company-sponsored hunts I used to get invited to before I became a has-been outdoor writer. Several other writers were there besides me: Jim Casada, Gary Sefton, Steve Hickoff, Jim Zumbo, Dodd Clifton, a few others.

I'd evidently been living right. I'd already taken good gobblers that spring on public land in Florida, Mississippi and Alabama. I was supposed to hunt with one of the camp's guides at Adobe, but he had a family emergency. Skipper apologized profusely, loaned me one of the camp trucks, drew a map in the dirt and left me to my own defenses. No problem; I hated it that my guide had troubles, but I really prefer to hunt alone. I drove to the parking spot, found the sendero Skipper said led away past the locked gate, and walked a half-mile in the cool

Courtesy of Gary Sefton.

Obviously, The Magic Roost wasn't the only productive place to hunt at Adobe that year. The third kneeling hunter from the left is Kristen Cole. To Kristen's left is another remarkable woman – Linda Powell, then of Remington and now of Mossberg. I'm proud to call them both my friends. And all these other turkey bums, too, of course.

Texas pre-dawn toward the roost Skipper told me was back in there somewhere.

I had no problem finding it. I heard 'em gobbling long before it got light enough to see, and the sheer quantity of the noise stopped me in my tracks. I disremember now what got them started – owl, coyote – but I'll never forget what they sounded like. Skipper told me there were multiple gobblers at the roost, but "multiple" means anything more than one. These being Rios, I was expecting five or six.

I confess to you now, I was unprepared for the cacophony of gobbling emanating from that roost. It sounded like gobbler central. It sounded like date night at a turkey farm. It sounded like half the gobblers in Texas had gathered for a gobbling contest, and every one of them was determined to finish in the money.

The roost was a live oak motte along the Middle Concho River, and it's always a gamble when you set up on roosted turkeys near a water barrier. The Middle Concho isn't much as rivers go, but it's not something I wanted to cross with full hunting gear if the turkeys went out the other way.

I'm a believer in minimal calling when gobblers are still on the limb; you already know that if you're this far along in this book. Overcalling tends to make them hang up in the tree and wait for the hen to come walking underneath. But that's with Easterns, and they don't normally roost in huge gatherings like the one I was dealing with here. With something like 35 or 40 gobblers hearing and responding to my calling, I figured at least one or two of them would fly down no matter how much I called, and I needed them to fly down my way. Jealousy and breeding season competition had to count for something, didn't it?

I'm also a believer in getting in tight on a roosted gobbler. I like to be no more than a hundred yards from the roost, closer if possible. In this situation, though, I thought it best to set up farther away. Killing a gobbler with a shotgun is a disruptive business – the shot, the flopping of the slain turkey, the mad dash to the flopper, the yelling and laughing and high-fiving and acting a fool. I generally do all my acting a fool stuff when I'm working the gobbler, not after I've shot him, and there wouldn't be any high-fiving since I was there by myself, and I got over all that mad dash-yelling-laughing crap when I saw on TV and videos how childishly stupid it looks.

But the shot and the flop were things I couldn't control. If I set up at 60 yards and there were 40 gobblers in that roost, 39 of them were going to be very close to a loud shotgun blast and would see number 40 doing his death dance right in their bedroom. I didn't want that to happen, so I backed off down a little open lane that led away from the roost and the river. At about the 200-yard mark, I found a perfect natural blind where the feathery limbs and leaves of a leaning mesquite formed a little cave with 20-inch-high grass out front. It came complete with a backrest provided by another mesquite that had quit leaning and given in to gravity. It too was still alive, and it provided further camouflage on the side of the blind nearest the roost.

Perfect. After carefully checking the ground on both sides of the grounded mesquite trunk (I'm not afraid of snakes, but this was prime rattlesnake country and I've been bitten and know from experience it's no fun) I sat down, thereby breaking my rule about getting in tight on my roosted gobbler. Then I broke the other rule about not calling much.

Not only did I break the don't-call-much rule, I threw it to the ground and stomped that sucker flat. I bet I called more in the next 20 minutes than I did the rest of the 2004 turkey season. It was, literally, nonstop. I ran a mouth call (actually two or three of them,) two pot-and-peg calls, two boxes (one of them the old Lohman box mentioned earlier,) a little Lynch Jet scratch box, a homemade Garret snuff can tube call, and a wingbone. I was better with some than others, but every sound I made got walked on by more gobblers than you could stuff into a motel hot tub.

Plucked.

And sure enough, jealousy and competition came into play. As far as I could tell, nobody hung up on the roost. The turkeys came down in waves. I could see part of the motte over the tops of the mesquite trees, and I saw four, then five more, then a wad I didn't have time to count, then more after that. Some of them went east across the Concho, but most pitched down on my side.

I didn't call any more after that. I didn't want to, because this was a remarkable morning and I didn't want to end it too soon. And I certainly didn't need to call; I had a dozen or more gobblers sounding off all around me, none of them farther than 150 yards. It was almost a mathematical certainty one of them would eventually walk up my lane. Thirty minutes after flydown, two of them did just that. I could have killed both, but I wanted to be sitting at that roost again the next morning.

The one I killed was a honker – 22 pounds, with 10 inches of bushy beard and 1-1/4 inch spurs. But I didn't know those statistics for a couple hours after the shot, because I sat there and listened to the remaining gobblers for that long before claiming my kill and walking happily back to the truck.

*   *   *

The next morning found me parking at the same locked gate, but not alone this time. The evening before, Skipper had asked me if I'd serve as guide for Kristen Cole, a personable young woman representing LaCrosse boots at the hunt. I was happy to oblige, on several levels. Kristen was a new young hunter and I've always enjoyed helping young people get started. She was also a manufacturer's rep, and outdoor writers are by necessity shameless brown-nosers around makers of outdoor equipment. I also wanted to show someone else this magnificent, mind-numbing turkey roost. And, not least, since when does a red-blooded male turn down a chance to hunt with an absolutely gorgeous young woman?

We walked the same sendero, but at a more leisurely pace this time because I now knew the lay of the place and knew where we needed to be and how long it took to get there. The turkeys weren't gobbling yet, but they got started about the time we reached the blind, and by the time we'd made the snake check, gone behind separate bushes to get rid of coffee, and took our seats in the blind they were in full roar. I could see the whites of Kristen's eyes in the gloom.

"How many turkeys is that?" she whispered. "This is more gobbling than I've heard in my life, all put together!" I knew how she

231

felt, because I'd felt it yesterday and was feeling it again this morning.

"I don't know. Maybe 30, maybe a million. For sure, it's one less than I heard here yesterday."

"Tomorrow it'll be less than that," she said. When she grinned her teeth flashed as white as her eyes, and I fell the rest of the way in love. A gorgeous, bloodthirsty turkey killer who works for a boot company? You would have, too.

I started calling to them again to get them leaning our way, but this time I didn't lay it on quite as thick. I quit calling and encouraged Kristin to take over, and she sounded pretty good on both a box and a slate. The gobblers thought so, too, and when they started pitching out I was able to count fourteen as they sailed out of the live oaks. There were quite a few more.

Kristen wanted me to take over the calling when they were down. I started once to stay quiet the way I'd done yesterday, but male ego took over and I wanted her to think I was a hot-shot turkey man. It was easy. We'd have had turkeys come to our set-up if I'd been playing a harmonica. Kristen had said she only wanted to shoot one gobbler because she also wanted to hunt again tomorrow, so we made up a game plan. If only one gobbler came in, it was to be her shot. If two or more came, she'd go first and I'd play mop-up.

Three came. But two of them stopped at 60 yards while the remaining bird closed the gap.

"Slight change of plan," I whispered. "You kill this one, but don't move after the shot. If he flops, they'll probably come investigate. You tell me when you're ready to shoot and I'll make him stop walking."

"I'm ready now," she said immediately. In the next second, four things happened:

I clucked.

Kristen shot.

The gobbler tipped over backwards.

The other two turkeys spun around and started running.

They were out of sight in a flash, but I came to my senses and hit a hard lick on my mouth call and they both gobbled. I hit them again and here they came back, not as fast as they left but fast enough. I let them close to 30 yards and shot the biggest-looking one when they stopped to look at their dead buddy.

The turkey went down but was right back up. I belted him again and he went back down. Got back up. Out of sight he went, flopping and limping badly.

"I'll be right back, I hope," said, and took off after him – the fat man's dash, with camo and shotgun. He was piled up dead when I rounded the corner of mesquite, and when I walked back with my bird, Kristen was standing over hers.

"He's so pretty I don't want to touch him," she said.

But when she did, I saw her eyes go round and wide for the second time that morning. For good reason, too. My gobbler was a fine one, almost as good as yesterday's bird, but Kristen's put mine to shame: 24 pounds, 11 inches of well rope, and needle-sharp daggers measuring an honest inch and a half each.

*   *   *

Both my tags were filled and I figured I was through hunting, but that evening Gary Sefton drew me aside.

"You seem to have the hot hand on this hunt. Would you mind taking Zumbo to that roost in the morning? He's had a rough two days hunting, and he needs a turkey bad."

How could I not? I've read Jim Zumbo's stuff since I was a teenager, and I delight in telling him that every chance I get because I know how much it annoys me when middle-aged men say it to me. Miss a chance to hunt with him? Hah. Not in this lifetime.

Walking in the next morning, I watched Jim's eyes get big and round like Kristen's had, but somehow the effect wasn't the same. He was as impressed as she and I had been, though. You couldn't tell the mob was down by three members, and they were already tearing it up when we left the truck.

I figured the mesquite blind might have become a no-fly zone to the survivors, so we picked a spot a couple hundred yards from the old spot and a little closer to the roost and the river. I also slacked off quite a bit more on the pre-flydown calling, thinking the turkeys might be wising up to that as well.

The roost serenade was just as lusty without my excessive calling, although when the gobblers flew down it seemed like more of them flew across the river. Still, we had quite a few turkeys to work with, and in short order a single longbeard came walking along a cattle track, straight toward us. Not strutting, just looking. He came to about 50 yards, stopped, then went back the way he came. I got him stopped at 90 yards, but he wouldn't come back.

After he was gone, another bunch of gobblers came in to about 80 yards, got all worked up and started fighting among themselves, after which they too drifted out of sight. We were watching two more gobblers strutting way off down a fencerow when a whole train of hens came trotting by us, towing four hopeful longbeards along. As it so often happens when there's only one shooter, I had the better angle and viewpoint.

"Are they longbeards?" Zumbo whispered. I said yes, but before he could make a move to get his gun up we both saw two big gobblers come in from the left to intercept the hens. They were better situated for Jim's right-shouldered field of fire, and the veteran hunter pulled off a snappy double, like they were mallards.

One weighed 23, the other 22. Heavy, impressive beards. Spurs commensurate with three-year-old gobblers. Not a bad wrap-up for The Magic Roost.

*   *   *

See, I told you this wasn't a Bad Bird story. I don't know what to call it, really. But in three mornings, I watched five trophy gobblers get subtracted from that roost, without making a detectable dent in the population. The smallest of the five weighed 21 pounds, the smallest beard was 10 inches and thick as a good Cuban cigar, and the spurs were, without exception, magnificent.

As enjoyable as that trip was, I'm actually glad experiences like that are rare. Turkey hunting is supposed to be tough. That's the whole point.

Chapter 29

The Friend of a Friend

This, like the chapter before it, is not a Bad Birds tale. Instead, it's a cautionary tale.

It's also a drastic swerve out of the normal, feel-good Bad Birds theme, because this story isn't so much about turkey hunting as it is about the honor, honesty and ethics surrounding turkey hunting. Or, in this case, the absence of those things. I apologize for that, but this story needs to be told.

It started on a promising note. Our new stockbroker – call him Hank, because it's not his name – was a nonhunter. But Hank was a nice guy, and he had another client, a friend since college, who was as consumed by turkey hunting as Jill and I. Hank's friend – call him Steven, because it *is* his name – owned a land development business that had treated him well, and with a portion of that wellness he had bought 550 acres of beautiful hardwoods in the rolling hill country of Holmes County, Mississippi, a few miles west of Lexington. Hank had invited Jill and me to meet him at Steven's place for a mid-April weekend hunt. Hank offered to serve as chief cook and bottle-washer while Steven, Jill and I hunted. Because of overcrowding and low turkey numbers, we'd given up on Mississippi public land, but 550 acres of prime private land was a different breed of cat. We accepted with both gratitude and anticipation.

Arriving late on Friday, we found Steven, cowboy hatted, wearing cut-offs and knee-high rubber boots, mowing the lawn on a small tractor. He was friendly and hospitable, and after we were squared away at the camp, our host took us on an electric buggy tour.

Steven had improved his property with the help of a generous checkbook, government cost-sharing programs and the savvy of a veteran outdoorsman. He created several fertile, good-sized ponds and stocked them. He built a roomy, comfortable lodge that was everything an outdoor enthusiast could want, with an equipment shed and climate-controlled barn to match. He cleared more than 20 food plots in strategic locations around the property. All this was linked together by a comprehensive but unobtrusive ATV trail network. We went through maybe half of Steven's food plots, about half of them containing elevated, tripod corn feeders. I asked Steven about it.

"Oh, those have been empty since deer season ended," Steven said. And sure enough, the two or three feeders we drove close to were empty with no corn on the ground anywhere. I didn't give it any more thought.

We spent an enjoyable evening – catching bass, eating good groceries and hearing entertaining stories from Hank's and Steven's college years – and then to bed. Two minutes later it was morning and time to hunt.

*   *   *

On Steven's advice, Jill and I drove to the back side of the property via county roads. We parked by a locked gate on the south property line, almost a mile south of the lodge. We walked a few hundred yards into the property on one of the ATV trails and stopped to listen at a fork, where a hand-lettered sign shaped like an arrow pointed to "The Tree House." Just as we reached the fork, a turkey gobbled in the direction the arrow was pointing.

That quick, the hunt was joined. We covered 150 yards and came to a reverse L-shaped food plot, and sure enough, a tall box stand was built amongst the branches of a big cherrybark oak at the outside corner of the L. The turkey was gobbling around the corner somewhere, and I eased up 40 yards to where I could see down that way. The other leg of the food plot was considerably longer and there was a downslope 50 yards away. The turkey was somewhere farther, beyond the slope and out of sight. The pitch of the downslope prevented me from seeing the rest of the plot. (Remember that detail, it will come into play shortly.) But if the treeline at the end was an accurate measure, the plot extended another 50 to 60 yards beyond the drop-off, and I didn't know if the turkey was in the food plot or in the woods beyond.

Either way, it would have been a risky move to try to see the end of the plot. I backed out, told Jill the lay of the land, and we decided to make our setup side by side and just short of the L in the food plot, on the short leg of the L but where we could see 15 yards around the corner. While we were getting into position the bird gobbled two or three more times from the same place, and I figured he was still on the limb. It was still pretty early, but Mississippi turkeys often fly down ahead of schedule when they have open ground to fly down in. He could be either aloft or grounded. We'd know soon enough.

Jill was getting ready to call to him – she does the soft stuff better than I do – when two things happened almost simultaneously: the turkey gobbled again, and a split-second later we heard, from behind us on the road we'd walked to the food plot:

"Game warden! I'm coming in. Unload your guns right now and lay them on the ground!"

It aggravated me a little; he'd heard the turkey gobble, and here he was messing up our hunt. If he wanted to check us, I thought, he could have done it after the hunt played out. We complied, of course; when you're in the turkey woods and a wildlife officer tells you to do something, you by God do it, and you do it right then. If you want to argue, argue later.

We laid our empty guns on the ground, barrels to the rear, and up the trail came a stern-looking, no-nonsense wildlife officer. Every part of his uniform was perfect: creases in his pants, spit-shined boots, the whole nine yards. His name tag read *Blaylock*, his rank insignia said Staff Sergeant. No rookie game warden here; my guess was former Marine.

As is my unattractive wont in nervous situations, I made a stab at humor: "Man, I'm sure glad I remembered to bring my hunting license this morning."

It fell flat.

"I need to see your licenses and turkey permits," Sergeant Blaylock said. No pleasantries, no smile. We produced them, and his frown deepened. Jill's license passed muster; as a former Mississippi resident, she'd bought a lifetime license before moving to Arkansas, and he was familiar with the license type. Mine, though, was different. The Mississippi Department of Wildlife, Fisheries and Parks has a special 7-day all-inclusive hunting and fishing license for media folks who come to the state for purposes of publicizing the outdoor opportunities available in the state, and that's what I handed the stern Sergeant Blaylock.

"Where's your turkey permit?" he asked, studying the unusual license with suspicion. "Where did you get this, anyway? I've never seen one like this before."

I explained that it was a special media license and that it was all-inclusive. "If you'd just call the…" but that was as far as I got.

"Mr. Spencer, I've been doing this job for 20 years. I think I know how to do it." There was true anger in his voice, and it puzzled me. Over a 60-year career of buying hunting and/or fishing licenses in 40-odd states and six countries, I'd had literally hundreds of encounters with wildlife officers. None had acted in such a hostile manner. We were perfectly legal – or so I thought.

"Sergeant, I'm not trying to be argumentative," I said, "but you're mad at us about something. Have we done something wrong?"

He looked at me like I had two heads. "Do you expect me to believe you don't know you're hunting over bait?"

I'm sure my jaw fell. "Bait? Where?" And right on cue, from the far end of the food plot (the part that couldn't be seen because of the downslope, remember?) came the distinctive, whirring rattle of an automatic feeder spewing out its allotted measure of corn.

Sergeant Blaylock inclined his head toward the sound and said, "You're telling me you didn't know that feeder was there." It wasn't a question.

But that was exactly what we were telling him. We did not know. But in the end it didn't matter anyway. Ignorance is not a valid excuse for breaking the law, and Jill and I erred by trusting the friend of a friend. We had not specifically asked Stephen if there were any active feeders on his property, nor did we check out the far end of the food plot because we'd have bumped the gobbler I now suspect was standing underneath that feeder. If we'd done either of those things, we might have had somewhere to stand and plead our case. But again: ignorance is no excuse.

I think Sergeant Blaylock believed us in the end, but he also did his job and wrote us four tickets: one to Jill for hunting with the aid of bait, and three to me for the bait violation and for not having a valid non-resident license and turkey tag. (Those last two citations were later invalidated when my license proved to be legal, but we paid the baiting tickets, $222 apiece. Now, at age 76, I have my very first wildlife violation. Thank you very much, Steven, you son of a bitch.)

Sergeant Blaylock, though, did tell us he had access to several pieces of private land in an adjoining county, and if we wanted to come back to Mississippi next year he could get us hunting privileges. "They don't bait turkeys on those places," he said, trying to suppress a grin. I didn't try to suppress mine. His attempt at humor was funnier than mine had been.

*   *   *

The jury is still out, but I think Jill and I might just take Sergeant Blaylock up on his offer. Once he decided we truly were acting out of ignorance rather than being deliberate poachers, his attitude softened and he seemed like the kind of guy you'd enjoy spending time with. And I'd hate for my four decades of Mississippi turkey hunting to end on a sour note.

Our weekend hunt at Steven's place, though, did end that way. I told him exactly what I thought about somebody who would knowingly send guests into a baited area without telling them. We packed our stuff in five minutes flat and were back home in the Ozarks before suppertime. I felt sorry for Hank, getting stuck in the middle through no fault of his own. But I suppose it proves the old adage that no good deed goes unpunished.

We're still friends with Hank and he's still our broker, but Steven? Not so much. That "friendship" lasted less than a day, and I wouldn't throw him a rope if he was stuck in a well.

Chapter 30

The Day Jim "Helped"

By Jill J Easton

Jim Spencer's note: Since the previous chapter was such a downer, I'm including this chapter, with my wife's permission, to bring the tone of the book back up where it ought to be. (Although, in the interest of full disclosure, my version of this same hunt has a decidedly different spin.)

Turkey hunts from purgatory. That's how I'd have described my turkey season so far. Birds gobbled and strutted at my best and worst calls but wouldn't even think about coming to me. Gobblers showed up in the wrong places, ran in the opposite direction and in general acted like I was wearing a red *Danger, Warning, Avoid At All Cost* sign around my neck.

Mississippi and Arkansas had been bad enough, but Missouri was worse. Was I calling too much? Using a slate when the birds wanted a box call? Were my calls all out of tune? I was out of ideas after running and rerunning everything in my turkey vest.

Jim had killed one in Mississippi, had filled both tags in Arkansas and now he'd tagged out early in Missouri. It was getting tedious, and so was he. Now he was hanging around camp, eating summer sausage and Osceola cheese, offering "helpful" comments about my turkey hunting and sneering from the sidelines. It was time to put the guy who wrote three books (now four) on turkey hunting to work.

The next morning, with both of us waiting at my favorite hunting spot, it started again. Gobbles north, south, east and west. Turkeys were everywhere.

I called. Spencer made some constructive comments. I stopped calling as he suggested. The gobblers went frantic; they were hammering from tree limbs in all directions as fast as they could get the notes out. We probably heard 300 gobbles in twenty minutes. Then they flew down, and, typical of my hunting experiences so far that spring, dead silence slammed down from every direction.

Finally, in the far distance a single gobble floated in on the morning breeze. Moments later we were sprinting up a mountain. Me with a gun, full backpack, and turkey decoys. Jim had water, a seat cushion and a cell phone camera. He outdistanced me. Duh. When I caught up we both were still panting and the turkey was still warbling its love song. Then the gobbling got louder, and we could hear the turkey drumming. My cool, calm, turkey-killing husband came apart like a styrofoam jetliner.

"He's coming! Sit! Sit down right here!" Jim whisper-yelled, grabbing my shoulder and shoving me toward a tree. *"That turkey is right over the crest of that hill. He's not 75 yards away. Get your gun up, stay calm, don't move. Get ready. Do it NOW!"*

Ten minutes late the turkey was still drumming and my husband was still panting, even though we'd been sitting ultra-still. This was a Jim Spencer I'd never witnessed before.

The drumming shifted direction. *"You're not pointed the right way! Aim over there!"* He grabbed me by the backpack and manhandled me in a slightly different direction. The panting was getting worse, and he was vibrating like an old four-wheeler on an Ozark mountain trail.

"Theturkeyisgoingtoshowuprightoverthere! Eyesopen!" Spencer whispered loudly, running his words together, stabbing his forefinger

at the woods like he was trying to spear the invisible turkey.

I was beginning to wonder if he was having a heart attack, or if he had maybe lost his mind over this bird. His agitation was getting me shaky. My gun barrel was wobbling up, down, sideways. My nerves were buzzing like flies around carrion.

"Thereheis,thereheis!" Jim sounded like a speed-freak version of Gollum in *The Hobbit*, fast talking but whispery. *"Move your gun to the left! He's coming. We won't call any more. Let him look for us."*

Sure enough, the turkey was doing what gobblers do when trying to impress a girl. His full tail fan was spread, catching coppery glints from the early-morning sun. His wings were dragging and shimmying and his head was pulled back in that tight S-curve that indicates the old man knows he looks darn handsome. The bird's beard was awesome. Even at 70 yards I could tell it was thick and long, and I was confident he had spurs to match. He was a big, mature gobbler that would impress everyone back at camp. *If* my near-berserk husband didn't screw it up.

The turkey stood still, drumming and strutting. Five minutes passed, and Jim couldn't stand the silence. He shifted his mouth call and hit a few soft notes. The turkey responded with a gobble that rattled at the end. He started closing in.

I was ready, gun on my knee. The turkey was angling sideways in full strut; each passing second brought it closer. Jim was vibrating like a plucked guitar string, but at least he had stopped whispering, whimpering and panting. I hoped.

Then it started again, the desperate, breathy voice in my ear.

"Herehecomes, herehecomes! Your gun isn't pointed right, get down on the barrel. NO! Don't move now, wait until the bird turns his back, then slide your gun over to the other knee." Spencer's voice was pitching higher and higher and the panting was starting again. The boy was in full, turkey-inspired meltdown.

The gobbler had moved within 60 yards, almost in range. He

was still strutting and gobbling every few turns, moving closer with each spin. His drumming was loud and strong.

"He's in range now, whenever you get a shot, take it," Spencer said after a bit, then immediately changed his mind. *"NO! Wait! I'll tell you when to shoot."*

By now I was as jangly as my partner, although my bounding gun barrel was under better control than his breathing.

Right here was where communications broke down.

"When I cluck, he'll put his head up, then you shoot."

That's what Spencer claimed he said. What I heard was, "SHOOT," and I did. The gobbler was in full strut and walking. Between those two things and a severe case of jitters I'd caught from my hunting "helper," I missed that turkey clean. The bird vanished before I could chamber another shell.

Spencer jumped up with a bonus case of the reds. He called me, turkeys and everything else in range unkind names. I stomped off, muttering unpleasantries under my breath. Fifteen minutes later, after we'd both calmed down and cooled off, he owled at me. I owled back, we hooked back up and headed out to look for another gobbler. We found one. I killed it. We were friends again.

But that's why I don't hunt with Jim anymore unless he's carrying a gun of his own. That boy just can't keep himself under control.

But when Jim does have a gun of his own, sometimes things work out better for this turkey hunting partnership. Not always. But sometimes.

Chapter 31

The Safety Man

The place is in the Deep South. That's all I'm going to tell you. It's at least 10,000 acres, probably more, and aside from food plots, ponds and a few smallish pastures it's one continuous block of beautiful hardwood timber, with a virtual mansion smack dab in the middle. Even the caretaker's "cabin" is far better than any house I've ever owned.

It's the poster-child property of hard labor, sweat equity and good old-fashioned Southern values, an estate put together over time by a blue-bib-overalled logger who worked his butt off and scrimped and saved and plowed most of his logging profits into buying more land and treating it well. It's managed primarily for deer, but they don't neglect the turkeys on the place, and the turkeys appreciate it.

In April 2015, via the convoluted paths created in a lifetime of being a dedicated turkey bum, I was lucky enough to be invited to hunt this Mecca. Mike Boykin, the caretaker, invited his neighbor Clark Dixon to hunt, and Clark got me invited as a tag-along to do the shooting while Clark played the role of cameraman.

I wish he hadn't brought that camera. Otherwise I could deny what happened.

Even though the property is immense, most of it is readily accessible because of an elaborate road network. The property is so big, though, it's been necessary to hang a series of orange wooden arrows at most of the road intersections so guests unfamiliar with the place can find their way out.

But since we had the head groundskeeper with us, we didn't need those orange signs. Nor, as it turned out, did we need vehicles. When we got to Mike's "cabin" before dawn that morning, he told us he'd heard a gobbler at sundown the evening before, within easy walking distance from his back yard. We gathered our gear, walked maybe 350 yards down one of those well-maintained interior roads and made out set-up at a three-way junction. One of the three ways led directly down a slight incline to where Mike had heard the gobbler last night.

It was a sweet set-up. Clark was to my left with his camera, at about 30 degrees. Mike was behind me and to the right, with his shotgun for back-up. I was against a tree where I could watch all three approach roads. The gobbler began his morning soliloquy right on schedule, and we were about 150 yards from him. He gobbled a goodly number of times on the roost, flew down at the normal time, and when Mike and I gave him a little soft stuff – Mike with a slate, me with a mouth call – he gobbled back. Two or three minutes later he gobbled again, and he was closer. I got my gun on my knee. Mike purred on his slate and the gobbler cut him off. I scrooched down on my cushion. Things were happening fast.

And then he was there, coming into view right over the bead of my shotgun barrel. I didn't have to move it an inch.

You were expecting another Bad Birds story, right? Sorry to disappoint you. This was shaping up to be one of the easiest hunts I'd ever had.

It would have been, too, if I hadn't managed to screw it up.

The gobbler was killable when I first saw his head, and when he stopped in the middle of the three-way intersection he was 27 yards from the end of my barrel. He was calm and he was looking for the hen. He never strutted, and I had the bead on his neck wrinkles, confident as Mark Twain's famous Christian with four Aces. I calmly watched the gobbler search for the hen, letting Clark get all the B-roll he wanted.

Eventually, though, a calm gobbler loses a little of that calmness when he fails to see the hen he expects to be standing there. I figured we had about reached that stage of the encounter, and my suspicion proved correct when the gobbler shook his shoulders and re-set his wings.

Okay, time to kill him. He was already erect and alert, so there was no need for the cluck that would raise his head. Just as he turned to leave, I tightened my trigger finger. And tightened. And tightened.

Nothing happened, except that I might have bent the trigger on my 870 a little bit. The gobbler was still standing in place but was clearly about to leave when I finally diagnosed the problem. Rather than using finger and thumb to ease the safety off, I stabbed at it like I was trying to kill a wasp, and it responded by saying CLICK!!! loud enough to hear it back at Mike's cabin.

It had the effect you'd expect. The motionless gobbler became a black blur, heading back down the road he'd come in on. I had 25 yards to get on him and kill him, and I could have more than likely pulled it off. But some years before this hunt took place, I vowed to quit shooting at running or flying gobblers, for the same reason legendary Texas Longhorns football coach Darrel Royal didn't like passing the football: "Three things can happen, and two of them are bad."

I didn't want to risk crippling a turkey, especially in front of my host, so I watched the turkey run out of my life forever. Then I stood, shook my head and laughed, and thereby earned the amazement of Mike Boykin.

"I've turkey hunted a long time and seen some stuff," he said, "but I never saw anybody laugh at themselves when they screwed up that bad." Thank you, Mike, for pointing that out to me. I hadn't noticed.

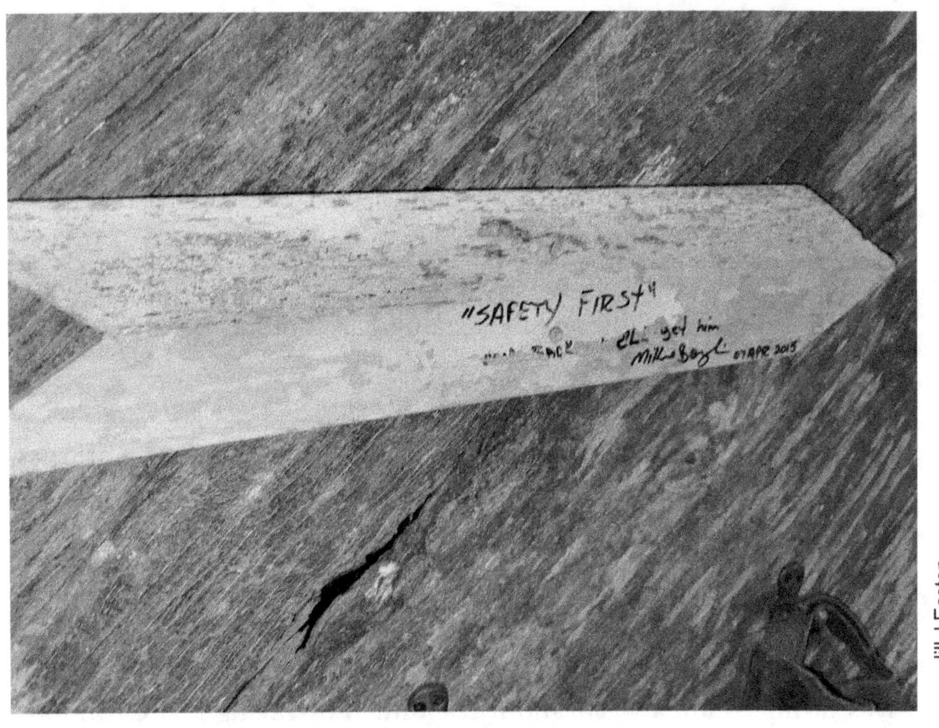

Clark, meanwhile, was having a giggle-fit beside his tree, and it took him a few minutes to get himself under control, gather up his camera stuff and join us on the road.

"Man oh man, I wouldn't have missed this hunt for the world!" he said, wiping tears out of his eyes. "That turkey went like this." And he mimicked, nearly perfectly, the gobbler standing erect, then turning and running, still erect, down the road. The second time he did it, I told him to do it one more time, so I could see if I could have hit that running gobbler. It stopped the demonstrations; it did not stop the giggle fits.

I never got a chance to redeem myself. Mike was tied up the next day, and the day after that Jill and I had to leave for a meeting.

But a month later, a package showed up in the mail. It was one of those orange wooden directional arrows. On it, Mike had written: "Safety First". Below that: "Come back we'll get him."

That orange arrow is tacked to the barnwood wall in our living room, not far from the "Spencer Special" mouth call mentioned in Chapter 5. I keep it there to remind me of several things: 1. When the time comes, take off the safety. 2. Don't get overconfident, even if it looks like a slam dunk. 3. And most important, it reminds me of friends.

Chapter 32

The Foggy Bottom Gobblers

It's an oddball land feature.

To begin with, it's flat as a one-egg cake, even though it's in the Ozarks and is surrounded on three sides by hillsides that give new meaning to the word "steep." It was at one time cleared and worked as a homestead farm; the stone foundations of the house and several outbuildings next to a good sized spring in the middle of the property attest to previous ownership. But the Depression changed all that, and the land has since reverted to a mixed hardwood forest. It's not a huge place, maybe 200 acres, bounded on the fourth side, the east side, by a good-sized river. This little chunk of overflow river bottom is privately owned, as is the steep terrain that hems it in. Almost every tree along the river wears a no trespassing sign, and during deer season there's a family member in there more days than not.

But the landowners aren't turkey hunters, and they let me hunt the place in exchange for some predator management trapping and keeping them well supplied with catfish. It's a good trade, and if there's a problem with trespassing I'm not aware of it. The property is four miles from the nearest boat ramp, and even the ramp itself is well off the beaten path.

And the property has turkeys. It's just my kind of place, except for one little glitch: The river running along the east boundary is a tailwater stream, with deep-water releases from two dams keeping it cold enough to support a year-round trout fishery. Because it's a big river, it can make its own weather, and one of those weathers is fog. The fog can happen any season of the year, but it's most common in the transition months of spring and fall. That's why I've always called the place Foggy Bottom.

We're not talking about those wispy, wimpy little drifts of mist you see on warm rivers at daylight. This is full-bore, gray-out, pull-your-car-to-the-side-of-the-road fog, and it pools up in this walled-in little bottom like you wouldn't believe. When you pair a wet-blanket fog like that with a four-mile boat ride *in the dark,* and then you have to start hunting in dense fog to boot, it considerably complicates a turkey hunt.

For one thing, it pretty much eliminates pre-season scouting. I could do it by approaching the little bottom from above, but the high ground is in different ownership and I don't have permission from that landowner. And to do it by boat involves that four-mile boat ride that takes at least an hour. So I don't scout it, which means that almost every time I hunt there it's like going to a brand-new place and getting there late.

*   *   *

During the COVID-wrecked spring of 2021, Arkansas and Missouri opened their season on the same day. Jill and I elected to hunt the Missouri opener, so it was the fifth day of the season before I got back home and went to Foggy Bottom. I anticipated the fog and allowed time for it, but still it was well past daylight when OnX told me I was at the upriver property boundary. I eased the boat to the river's edge and located a good landing place where I could tie off and get up the bank. When I shut off the motor, two turkeys were gobbling downriver, still on land I could hunt but not far from the property line.

I'd forgotten to wear a rain jacket and was wet as a muskrat from motoring through the dense fog, but it was a mild morning and I was chilly but not cold. The walk downriver warmed me quickly, and because it was so foggy the gobblers were still on the roost.

I was pleased at where they were – hard against the riverbank, most likely in one of the dozen huge streamside sycamores that flanked the river along the lower property line. The gobblers wouldn't fly across the river because of the fog. The high ground on the downstream side of the bottom had them hemmed in on the south, the river had them on the east, and I didn't think they'd pitch upstream because they had that line of big sycamores to fly through if they did. That left a westerly, away-from-the-river fly-down as the most likely thing, and in my infinite wisdom that's where I was. I wasn't smug, exactly – over the fullness of time, turkeys have a way of knocking that feeling out of you – but I felt pretty good about my chances.

The fog was persistent and they stayed in the trees for a long time that morning. As it turned out, I could have waited at the boat ramp until daylight and still gotten there in plenty of time. It was still foggy at 8 a.m. and by then the two turkeys had combined to gobble, oh, I don't know – maybe a million times?

Probably not quite that many, but I do know I was getting tired of hearing it, and that's never happened to me before or since. It was a *lot* of gobbling. I'd been sitting there for almost three hours and had yet to make a call. I was scared to; I was afraid it would make them stay in the tree even longer. I'd been there more than long enough for my butt to get numb, so before it lost all feeling I stood up and walked around my tree a few times to get the circulation going again.

I was on the fourth or fifth revolution when the sound of heavy birds leaving the limb reached my ears. I was on the back side of the tree from my stuff, including my gun, and I peered around the trunk just in time to see the two gobblers land 35 yards out. They were in perfect position for a shot, but I was in an impossible situation to deliver it.

I didn't even have my mask pulled up. All I could do was a sideways Kilroy impression, peering around the trunk to hide my white beard, gawking at the now silent but strutting turkeys.

I didn't dare call, but for a different reason now: they were so close I didn't want to call attention to myself. My only chance at turning this fiasco around was for them to walk far enough away for me to get to my gun and then call them back, a scenario so far-fetched it made me smile.

These were both very good gobblers, and under different circumstances I'd have enjoyed the show. But I was bent over at an uncomfortable angle, and after 10 minutes my back was telling me about it. I was trying to work out some sort of play when the gobblers saved me the trouble. One of them slicked down and started pecking at the ground and slowly walking straight at me, and in a few seconds the other bird followed his lead. They closed the gap to 30 yards, then 25, as I helplessly hid behind my tree. At 20 yards I quit looking at the whole turkeys and concentrated instead on their feet. Making eye contact with an in-your-face gobbler is a good way to induce panic in the gobbler, and, absurd as it now seems, I still had hopes I'd be able to snatch a victory out of this mess.

Nope. As it turns out, when a gobbler is close enough (five yards, in this case,) eye contact with an apex predator is not a requirement for spooking him. I don't know what set them off, but one second they were pecking contentedly along and the next they were in full-blown escape mode. The front gobbler flew, throwing wet leaves in my face with the force of his wingbeats. The other one swapped ends so fast I didn't even see it happen, and within a second or two I was peeking around a tree, looking at the big hole in Foggy Bottom left by the departed gobblers.

I walked around the tree and sat down where I should have been sitting the whole time. *I've screwed up a lot of turkeys in a lot of imaginative ways,* I remember thinking. *But that one takes the cake.* I sat there a while longer, ate a package of cheese crackers and drank some water. Thinking about my options.

I could go back to the boat and try a couple other places I had permission to hunt along this stretch of the river. I could go back to the boat and go fishing; there were two spinning rods and a tackle box in the boat. I could go back to the boat, go back to the landing, drive to the nearby national forest and try to find a late-morning bird. I could go back to the boat and quit for the day. That last one was out of the question, of course; turkey seasons are too short as is, and I have too few of them left in front of me to pout and waste half a morning just because I did something stupid.

So in the end I exercised none of those options. The two gobblers were obviously connected, or they wouldn't have gobbled so much and stayed side by side after flydown. They didn't know what had spooked them; I don't think they saw me so much as sensed my presence. (I am convinced turkeys can do that.) And since turkeys, like almost all wild creatures, live in the moment, I figured they were already largely calmed down from their panic attack and would soon be thinking about getting back together.

I gave them another 30 minutes, during which time the last of the morning fog lifted and dissipated. The sun streamed on a slant through the damp, half-grown leaves on the trees. The woods were a sharp contrast of stark shadow and brilliant golden sunlight. It had turned into a gorgeous morning.

*   *   *

The flying gobbler had gone west, straight away from the river. The runner had gone southeast, downstream in the direction of the high ground. I split the difference, went southwest until I came to the start of the high ground, and built a little blind against a fallen hackberry, using a few deadfall limbs to break up my outline. I was a little over 40 yards from the abrupt break between Foggy Bottom and the steep slope. I waited another 20 minutes after crawling into my hidey-hole, then unleashed a trio of slow, hoarse gobbler yelps.

Nothing happened. I waited 20 more minutes, did it again. Same result. It was now almost 11 o'clock. I settled back into my blind and got comfortable.

Maybe a little too comfortable. What woke me up was a hard-edged, questioning cluck from very close by. I worked my eyeballs back and forth in a slow scan of the forest in front of me, and I was halfway through the second slow sweep when the gobbler clucked again. Directly behind me. The hackberry log I was leaning against had a bow in it, and the bow raised the center of the log a little above shoulder height. That's where I'd made my blind, and that decision made any attempt to swing my gun around a fool's errand. But I could swing my head around to see back that way, and slow as molasses I made that move. One of the gobblers was standing not quite directly behind me, but close to it, at maybe 25 yards. It was hard to judge the distance with only one eyeball on him, and that one only peripherally. I knew two things for sure, though: he was killable, and I wasn't going to kill him. He stood there tall and pretty, and I sat there twisted like an arthritic pretzel.

I had cranked my head far past the point of comfort, and I desperately needed to uncrank it. Since there was no need to continue watching a gobbler I couldn't kill, I began the slow process of turning my head back to the front. About halfway through the reverse move, he clucked a third time, but this time it was more like an alarm putt. Sometimes it's hard to tell the difference, but not this time. He did it three or four more times in rapid succession, and the Doppler effect made each one softer as he quick-walked away, going uphill and off the property I could hunt. The benches above me weren't so much benches as they were ledges, with narrow flats separated by cow-faced slopes composed mostly of chunk rock. I wouldn't have gone after him even if I'd had permission.

Strike two. I sat there grumpy as a butt-shot bear, ignoring the beauty of the spring morning and the greening river bottom, Monday-morning quarterbacking my game plan. I'd stood up at the first set, okay, got that, but I couldn't think of a thing I could have done to improve my second play, except maybe to have stayed awake. I looked at my watch. 12:30.

*   *   *

At 1:30 I was still sitting there. That's when the turkey that had run downriver sent out a lonesome-sounding gobble, and I scrambled to grab my box call and give it a shake. I absolutely hate doing that; it's so amateurish, and to my ear at least, shaking a box call sounds about as much like a gobble as a mallard sounds like a wood duck. But I didn't want to cluck at him because that's what I'd done earlier.

He seemed to think it sounded okay, though, because two minutes later he gobbled again and this time he was closer. Hmmm. I shifted a little to my right to put the turkey at 45 degrees, slipped a mouth call in, and settled my gun on my right knee.

I saw him at 125 yards, walking slowly along the edge where flat ground met hillside. If he kept doing that, he'd walk within 42, maybe 43 yards. Close enough.

Which he didn't do, of course. Walk along the edge, I mean. He was still 50 yards from where I needed him to be when he started angling up the hill at a little notch where the slope was a little less forbidding. That put him 70 yards from the gun, and he was out of sight before he climbed five yards. He appeared again at the edge of the first bench, almost directly above me now but still 60 yards away. I'd moved my gun barrel in anticipation of him doing that, but he was too far and I knew it. He stood there like a king contemplating his domain, then gobbled again.

His buddy gobbled back, three or four benches straight up the mountain. He disappeared, and they gobbled themselves back together in short order. It was 2:15.

They continued to gobble intermittently, and it seemed like they were staying on about the same level as they worked their way to my right along the curve of the mountain. If they continued, they would eventually circle around the flat land and come back to the river at the upper end of it.

I didn't have any other options at the moment, so I cut across the bottom until I was at the upstream edge, where the river curved away from the mountain and created Foggy Bottom. I could still hear the turkeys gobbling on the mountainside, so I struggled up to the third bench (that was where I hit the property line) and started moving back toward the turkeys. I stopped when they were still about a quarter-mile away. I needed to know which bench they were on, and I didn't want to call to them until I was certain.

One of them gobbled again. Sounded like we were on the same bench; time to sit. This third bench was wider than the two I'd climbed to reach it, which is probably why the gobblers were on it. It was still only 60 to 70 yards wide, though, narrow enough for me to cover the entire width if I could find a set-up near the middle.

I did find one, and it was surprisingly comfortable despite all the rocks. The turkeys were gobbling every five minutes or so, both solo and as a duet, and by the time I was comfy they were 350 yards out and it was 3:20.

I wanted to just sit there quietly, let them amble along the bench to me, and bust one of them upside the head. That's what I really wanted to do. Looking back on it now, the situation reminded me of the story Blue Collar Comedy member Ron White used to tell about a confrontation he had with police outside a bar: "At that point, I had the right to remain silent. But I didn't have the ability."

Neither did I, and therefore I trotted out one of my more spectacular displays of turkey hunting idiocy. With two gobblers ignorant of my presence gobbling every five minutes and closing at a rate of five yards per minute, I waited until one of them gobbled again, then yelped softly on a Darrin Dawkins box.

Darrin makes some fine box calls, but like Ron White also said, "You can't fix stupid." That one little run of yelps hung those two gobblers up like somebody had roped them to a tree. They kept gobbling, but all forward progress stopped. Damage already done, I switched to more aggressive stuff, first using the Dawkins box, then my old Lohman box, then a Battey slate, then a raspy cutter mouth call, then on all of them mixed together in an enthusiastic gobbler fight. Somebody watching me might have thought I was fighting yellowjackets. I did everything but throw out a bushel of corn and holler "Here, turkey turkey turkey!"

It lit the turkeys up pretty good, and after I finally shut up they started moving again. But instead of continuing along the bench to me, they moved up one bench and came in above me. They did the predictable thing: came along the bench, out of sight and gobbling up a storm. They even got into a little bit of a dust-up, from the sound of it. Caught up in all the excitement, I suppose. But when they got directly above me they stopped moving again and just sat up there gobbling and drumming. They were in easy shotgun range and I was ready to do my part.

The closest I came to getting to do it was when I caught a glimpse of one of the tail fans. Just the tips of the three or four middle feathers, you know. The ones about four inches above a strutting gobbler's head. The ones that have no bone or blood vessels, so it would do a fella absolutely no good to shoot them. Which is what I desperately wanted to do.

Then the feather tips disappeared, and in a little while, so did my fit of madness.

The gobbling was slowly winding down. Ditto the drumming. I made one last cut-gobble-yelp jamboree. They gobbled a few more times, and I pulled the shotgun back into the hollow of my shoulder a little tighter. Somebody was going to peek over the edge of that bench. I knew it. I knew it.

Since we seem to be vested in quotes in this tale, let me adjust one from President Ronald Reagan: "It's not that turkey hunters aren't smart, it's just that so much of what they know isn't so."

The next time they gobbled, they were 150 yards past me, heading around the curve of the mountain toward the river. Strike three.

*   *   *

It was 4:45. I didn't have anywhere else to go, and the afternoon was pleasant. I went back to the boat, drifted with the current the three-quarters of a mile to the lower end of the property, and caught five eating-sized rainbows in the process. Now it was 5:45, and I was abreast of the line of sycamores where the gobblers had roosted that morning. The morning that seemed a century ago.

I tied off, climbed the bank, and set up against the northernmost sycamore. I'd sunk to a new low; if those two turkeys came back to roost in those sycamores, I was going to bushwhack one of them and lie like hell about it when I got back to civilization. I knew the gobblers were upstream, and I figured if they came back to the sycamores they'd come along the slightly higher ground of the river bank. Six-thirty came and went, and the mountain was throwing some deep shade. Visibility in the dense woods was poor. At 6:45 I decided to give up – and that's when the two turkeys gobbled 250 yards away. Straight upriver. I grinned like a monkey and put my gun on my knee.

Five minutes later they were there, less than 100 yards away, walking and pecking their way to me. They seemed to have not a care in the world except the one they didn't know about. The one that was sitting under their roost tree. The one that was pointing a shotgun at them. I didn't care which one I killed, so I lined up on the lead gobbler.

The important thing was that one of them die on this day.

Eighty yards. *Okay, get your head down on the gun. Quit trying to look over the barrel.*

Seventy yards. *Snick! went the safety.*

Sixty yards. *Get the bead on his head.*

Fifty. *Position the mouth call to make that last cluck that will stop him in his tracks.*

Forty. *Make sure your cheek is on the stock and you're looking down the barrel, not over it. You know how you are.*

Thirty-five. *Now, make the cluck.*

Thirty. *Maybe you didn't hear me. I said, make the cluck.*

Twenty-five: *Make the damned cluck, you fool!*

*   *   *

The first gobbler walked past me at 18 yards. The second one did, too. I reset the safety, turned my head and watched them go. They craned their necks curiously when they strolled past my boat 50 yards downstream, but didn't seem alarmed. They piddled around on the ground for a few minutes, then flew up three sycamores past the boat.

I sat there for a while, then got up and unloaded my gun. I walked along the edge of the water to the boat, shoved off as quietly as possible, and floated silently past where they had flown up. I couldn't see them.

I drifted another 200 yards downriver, then started the outboard and idled across to the east shoreline before twisting the throttle open and heading back to the landing. I drove home and pan-fried five rainbow trout for a late supper for Jill and me. Jill didn't understand why it was important that we eat them that night, but she's used to my weirdnesses so she dug in. There wasn't a speck of those fish left when we pushed back from the table, and the bottle of Chenin Blanc I'd opened met the same fate.

In these three Bad Birds volumes, I have taken you with me on 104 Bad Birds experiences. That number includes this tale. I've had more Bad Birds encounters than that, but for various reasons they wouldn't make good stories.

So, in all probability, this is the last Bad Birds piece I will ever write. That's appropriate, because these are the two Bad Birds I'm proudest of.

Epilogue

In the waning days of the 20th century, I bounced an idea off the noggin of my good friend Brian Lovett, who at the time was editor of *Turkey & Turkey Hunting* magazine. At the time, I'd been hunting turkeys for more than two decades. That whole time, I'd been a sort of walking pinata for what appeared to be an endless succession of ornery turkeys. I figured if the beatings were going to continue I might as well profit from them, so I told Brian I wanted to write a series of short stories about turkey hunting, each one starring a different difficult turkey I'd had personal experience with. I suggested a standing title for the series: *Bad Birds.*

I guess I caught Brian in a weak moment, because he jumped on it like a poult on a field cricket. A Bad Birds story has appeared in every issue of that magazine since. As of August, 2023, that's 74 issues and counting. Over the years, I hope you've enjoyed reading these tales of triumph and woe even half as much as I've enjoyed experiencing the hunts that inspired the narratives.

You might have noticed something different about most of the Bad Birds tales in this third book, though. Most of the chapters are longer. That's because only one of these chapters (Chapter 1, The Orchard Tender) has appeared in print. All the other Bad Bird episodes in this book are brand new stuff, never before published. Most of them are longer stories because I had limited space in the magazine, room enough for only 1200 words or so. That's not a lot, and I had to write pretty tight to get the story told.

Not so with the for-the-book-only BB chapters. I had space to stretch my legs, and even pontificate a little here and there. I've tried to stay off the soapbox as much as possible, but there's some of it in here. If any of it offends you…well, sorry about that.

But mostly, this book contains turkey stories. They all have happy endings, but some are happy for me and others are happy for the turkeys. I don't know how many of the Bad Birds in this book got killed, and how many times the turkeys lived to fool other hunters in other hunts. I suspect it's about a 60-40 ratio in the gobblers' favor.

But the thing is, I don't care. In every one of these stories, and in every one of the other turkey hunts I've made that never got written

Continued, page 270

Turkey hunting has blessed me in so many ways. One of the best of those blessings has been the many, many friends I've made over a lifetime of chasing these grand, aggravating birds for nearly a half-century. Here are two – Dale Causey (left) and Andy Terrell. These two south Mississippi gentlemen have been cherished friends for many years, and we met, literally, in the turkey woods. I know if I called either of them in the middle of the night and said I needed help, the only question they'd ask would be "Lawyers, guns or money?" They are only two of a multitude who would do the same thing. I can't list everybody here, but this is a sampling: Ken, Jim, Gary, Rob, Brad, Monte, Michael, Manuel, Colonel, David, Pete, Steve, Mark, Mike, Toxey, Bill, Jason, Cuz, Kevin, Omer, Harold, Steve again, Bobbie, Jason again, Ralph, Alan, Jill, Tommy, Doc, Tony, Tes, Bo, Jolly, Ken, Tammy, Bob, Randy, Brian, Shirley,.....well, you see where this is going, and if you're a member of this group you already know it, anyway. Thank you. I can't say it enough. Thank you. I wrote in the final pages of Bad Birds 2 that my life has been enriched by the pursuit of wild turkeys, but that was a little off the mark. The truth is, my life has been enriched by the many good friends I've met during the pursuit of wild turkeys. Like Augustus said to Woodrow: "It's been a hell of a party."

about, I've been the winner. I've been the winner because I was out there amongst 'em, I was a player in this game I love above all others. Every time. Every. Single. Time. That's worth something, you know?

Two years ago, I went through all my turkey hunting logbooks and added up all the days I've hunted turkeys. I forget the exact number, but it was somewhere north of 1200 days. Add the total from the last two seasons and I can with some confidence claim 1300 days in the spring turkey woods. That's a lot of wins. I am a fortunate man.

More accurately, I am a fortunate *old* man, and so this book is my swan song as a turkey writer. I expect I'll still have a story or two in the odd outdoor magazine from time to time, but I think this Bad Birds thing has run its course. I don't have enough turkey seasons left to accumulate enough material for a Bad Birds 4 – although I'm sure there are a lot of old longbeards out there who are willing to volunteer.

So, adieu. I want to thank you for being a reader of my stuff over the years. You are the sole reason I've been able to pile up those 1300 wins. It's been a good run, and it's not finished just yet. If we cross paths in the turkey woods some future day, let's do what Jill suggested in her foreword way back in the front of this book: Let's stop and sit on a log for a few minutes and swap a story or two. I'd like that.

Thank you again. I appreciate your patronage more than you will ever know.

Call 'em close.